CAMP NOTES AND OTHER WRITINGS

CAMP NOTES
AND OTHER WRITINGS

Mitsuye Yamada

RUTGERS UNIVERSITY PRESS
New Brunswick, New Jersey, and London

Camp Notes and Other Poems was originally published by Shameless Hussy Press in 1976 and by Kitchen Table: Women of Color Press in 1992. *Desert Run: Poems and Stories* was originally published by Kitchen Table: Women of Color Press in 1988. First published in one volume by Rutgers University Press in 1998.

Library of Congress Cataloging-in-Publication Data

Yamada, Mitsuye.
    [Camp notes and other poems]
    Camp notes and other writings / Mitsuye Yamada.
        p. cm.
    Originally published separately: Camp notes and other poems. San Lorenzo, Calif. : Shameless Hussy Press, c1976; and Desert run. Latham, NY : Kitchen Table: Women of Color Press, c1988.
    ISBN 0-8135-2606-X (pbk. : alk. paper)
    1. Japanese American women—Literary collections. 2. Japanese Americans—Literary collections. I. Yamada, Mitsuye. Desert run. II. Title.
PS3575.A4C3 1998
811'.54—dc21   98-35219
                                                                 CIP

British Library Cataloguing-in-Publication Data is available.

Calligraphy by Yoshikazu Yamada
Manufactured in the United States of America

Camp Notes
and Other Poems

For my mother, Hide.
In memory of my father, Jack.
And for Yosh and our children
Jeni, Phil, Steve, Kai, Hedi
and all sansei and yonsei
who keep us alive.

TABLE OF CONTENTS

III   OTHER POEMS

I. MY ISSEI PARENTS
TWICE PIONEERS
NOW I HEAR THEM

母が今言ふ事
其内に分つて来る、

WHAT YOUR MOTHER TELLS YOU

haha ga ima yu-koto
sono uchi ni
wakatte kuru

What your mother tells you now
in time
you will come to know.

□

GREAT GRANDMA

great
grandmama's savings
in boxed dividers:
colored stones
yellowed yarns
pine cones
fabric scraps
brown bags pressed
dried seaweeds
parched persimmons
bitter melon seeds
powdery green tea
leaves

life's allotment
she'd say
when used up
time to die

☐

MARRIAGE WAS A FOREIGN COUNTRY

I come to be here
because
they say I must
follow my husband

so I come.

My grandmother cried:
you are not cripple
why
to America?

When we land the boat full
of new brides
lean over railing
with wrinkled glossy pictures
they hold inside hand
like this
so excited
down there a dock full of men
they do same thing
hold pictures
look up and down
like this
they find faces to
match pictures.

Your father I see him on the dock
he come to Japan to marry
and leave me
I was not a picture bride
I only was afraid.

□

HOMECOMING

from Tillie Olsen

I widow
redo my life
scratch out lies
lie buried inside
the house all the time
sorrows my nights
cries still survive.

You child
chide me too
often look cross
eye not see me cry
alone widow after thirty-five
years have final right to live.

My first born your brother
all the time in my arms
cry his scrotum swell
screech in my ears
I cry alone
no sleep for me.

My second born
a son too
sickly brothers
born so close
together we cry
there was no one
else.

I was sick with you
soon to come
Papa say go home
to your mother in Japan
you born there
but my boys need me at home

in America
I must leave you there
with wet nurse
we send for you
later nothing else to do.

You only a girl
do not know what I suffer
you blame me too
much sickness in you
when you come home to us
we take you to hospital
at home I have two sons
your father and no help
no night nurse I
stay up with you
whine after me
when I leave.

Loving you
could not know
what pains to live
without love
my friend kill
herself hang
her family with eight children
don't know
how she could
do it for good reason
I think of her often
bring me comfort.

So little you run
home everyday after school
because there you hope
to find Mama
alive.

□

A BEDTIME STORY

Once upon a time,
an old Japanese legend
goes as told
by Papa,
an old woman traveled through
many small villages
seeking refuge
for the night.
Each door opened
a sliver
in answer to her knock
then closed.
Unable to walk
any further
she wearily climbed a hill
found a clearing
and there lay down to rest
a few moments to catch
her breath.

The village town below
lay asleep except
for a few starlike lights.
Suddenly the clouds opened
and a full moon came into view
over the town.

The old woman sat up
turned toward
the village town

and in supplication
called out
Thank you people
of the village,
if it had not been for your
kindness
in refusing me a bed
for the night
these humble eyes would never
have seen this
memorable sight.

Papa paused, I waited.
In the comfort of our
hilltop home in Seattle
overlooking the valley,
I shouted
"That's the *end?*"

□

遠慮

ENRYO

Enryo is a Japanese word
which sounds like
in leo.
What does being in a lion
have to do with humility
I asked Papa
who said
could be
since lions are
by tradition
regally proud
ENRYO is pride
in disguise.

Even so
it is holding back
saying no
thank you
saying no
trouble at all.

□

DIALOGUE

I said

Don't
after twenty years
you know
she's leaving
you
must listen to
her
stop
and listen.

He said

But I did
I called her in here
I asked
her
I hear
you have something
on your mind
WHAT
but she stood right
there
dumb
looking out
the window.

☐

II. CAMP NOTES

EVACUATION

As we boarded the bus
bags on both sides
(I had never packed
two bags before
on a vacation
lasting forever)
the *Seattle Times*
photographer said
Smile!
so obediently I smiled
and the caption the next day
read:

Note smiling faces
a lesson to Tokyo.

☐

ON THE BUS

Who goes?
Not the leaders of the people
combed out and left
with the FBI.
Our father
stayed behind
triple locks.
What was the charge?
Possible espionage or
impossible espionage.
I forgot which.

Only those who remained
free in prisons
stayed behind.

The rest of us went to
Camp Harmony
where the first baby
was christened

Melody.

□

HARMONY AT THE FAIR GROUNDS

Why is the soldier boy in a cage
like that?
In the freedom of the child's
universe
the uniformed guard
stood trapped in his outside cage.
We walked away from the gate and
grated guard
on sawdusted grounds
where millions trod once
to view prize cows
at the Puyallup Fair.

They gave us straws to sleep on
encased in muslin ticks.
Some of us were stalled under grandstand
seats
the egg with
parallel lines.

Lines formed for food
lines for showers
lines for the john
lines for shots.

☐

CURFEW

In our area
was a block head
who told us
what's what
in a warden's helmet.

Turn off your lights
it's curfew time!

I was reading
with a flashlight
under my blanket
but the barracks boards
in the hot sun
had shrunk slyly
telling
bars of light

Off with your lights.

There must be no light.

☐

IN THE OUTHOUSE

Our collective wastebin
where the air sticks
in my craw
burns my eyes
I have this place to hide
the excreta and
the blood which
do not flush down
nor seep away.

They pile up
fill the earth.

I am drowning.

☐

MINIDOKA, IDAHO

In Minidoka
I ordered a pair of white
majorette boots
with tassels from
Montgomery Ward
and swaggered in
ankle deep dust.

I heard
bullsnakes were sprinkled
along the edges
to rid us of dread
rattlers.
A few of their orphans
hatched and escaped behind
barbed wires
befriended by boys
with mayonnaise jars.

Let them go I said to Joe
they will poison us.
But they are lost, and see? Blind
said Joe.
We rescued them
from the bullies.

☐

BLOCK 4 BARRACK 4 "APT" C

The barbed fence
protected us
from wildly twisted
sagebrush.
Some were taken
by old men with gnarled
hands.
These sinewed branches
were rubbed and polished
shiny with sweat and body oil.

They creeped on
under and around our coffee table
with apple crate stands.

Lives spilled over us
through plaster walls
came mixed voices.
Bared too
a pregnant wife
while her man played *go*
all day
she sobbed alone
and a barracksful
of ears shed tears.

□

DESERT STORM

Near the mess hall
along the latrines
by the laundry
between the rows of
black tar papered barracks
the block captain galloped by.
Take cover everyone he said
here comes a twister.

Hundreds of windows
slammed shut.
Five pairs of hands
in our room
with mess hall
butter knives
stuffed
newspapers and rags
between the cracks.
But the Idaho dust
persistent and seeping
found us crouched
under the covers.

This was not
im
prison
ment.
This was
re
location.

☐

INSIDE NEWS

A small group
huddles around a contraband
radio
What?
We
are losing the war?
Who is we?
We are we the enemy
the enemy is the enemy.

Static sounds and we
cannot hear.
The enemy is confused
the enemy is determined
and winning.

Mess hall gossips
have it that
the parents
with samurai morals
are now the children.

☐

THE WATCHTOWER

The watchtower
with one uniformed
guard
in solitary
confined in the middle
of his land.

I walked towards the hospital
for the midnight shift.
From the rec hall the long body
of the centipede
with barracks for legs
came the sound of a
live band playing
Maria Elena
You're the answer to my dreams.
Tired teenagers
leaning on each other
swayed without struggle.

This is what we did with our days.
We loved and we lived
just like people.

☐

RECRUITING TEAM

Returning from the hospital
on duty all night
I stopped to watch a curious crowd
around two Army uniforms
old men shouting from their fringes
Baka ya ro nani yutto ru ka
Dumbbells! We don't believe you!
Inside circle listening
outside circle shouting
Bakani suruna
Don't make fools of us.
A bent spoon hit me
on the head.
I swung around and saw
I saw hundreds of fixed eyes
listening and not listening
to voices
beating
signals in the desert.

I put my hands over
my ears and
ran
but one
lone
voice
pursued me:

Why should I volunteer!
I'm an American
I have a right to be
drafted.

☐

P.O.W.

I sit
inside these fences
and forget
all my miseries
were left outside.

☐

My daily routine
of going to the mess hall
has nothing to do with
my appetite.

☐

—Jakki

Jakki was the penname of my father, Jack Yasutake,
formerly an interpreter for the Immigration Service, who
was interned by the FBI during the years 1941-1944.
These are translations of two of his senryu poems.

SEARCH AND RESCUE

We joined the party
for the feel of freedom.
What are we looking for
among gnarled knuckles
in sagebrush forest?

> An old man
> out of his head
> wandered off they said.
> We're scouts
> to help him across the gate.

In a straight line
we inched over
his twisted trail.
Is he bio
degradable
half buried in desert dust?

> He must be degraved,
> pulled up, potted, niched
> up against the stone wall.
>
> Enshrined.

□

THE TRICK WAS

The trick was
keep the body busy
be a teacher
be a nurse
be a typist
read some write some
poems
write Papa in prison
write to schools
(one hundred thirty-three colleges
in the whole United States in the back
of my Webster's dictionary
answered: no admittance
THEY were afraid of ME)

But the mind was not fooled.

☐

SOME PEOPLE WALKED THROUGH

Some people walked through
and out the back of my mind.

I'll bet you a home-made apple pie
you'll never get out of here in
a hundred years.
    That's impossible.
    Where in the world would you
    get apples?
Okay then I'll bet you
a million dollars.

What a pretty garden you made, *Obasan*.
    No, this is not much.
    The one I had in Seattle had
    many beautiful flowers.
Too bad we are not in Seattle.
    Sore wa shikata ga ari masen ne?
    That can't be helped can it?

What's your name?
    Bo ya
Whose boy are you?
    Nobody's
(Pinned on his back was a sign:
Please do not feed me.)

□

MESS HALL DISCIPLINE

The mother drew my eyes
to her smiling mouth
but still I saw her
pinch her daughter who let drop
the handful of mushy beans
shrieked a soundless cry
and abundant tears.

☐

THE QUESTION OF LOYALTY

I met the deadline
for alien registration
once before
was numbered fingerprinted
and ordered not to travel
without permit.

But alien still they said I must
foreswear allegiance to the emperor.
For me that was easy
I didn't even know him
but my mother who did cried out
    If I sign this
    What will I be?
    I am doubly loyal
    to my American children
    also to my own people.
    How can double mean nothing?
    I wish no one to lose this war.
    Everyone does.

I was poor
at math.
I signed
my only ticket out.

□

From 1942 to 1945 Japanese American internees were
expected to sign what came to be known as "The Loyalty
Oath" before leaving camp for eastern sections of the
United States.

THE NIGHT BEFORE GOOD-BYE

Mama is mending
my underwear
while my brothers sleep.
Her husband taken away by the FBI
one son lured away by the Army
now another son and daughter
lusting for the free world outside.
She must let go.
The war goes on.
She will take one still small son
and join Papa in internment
to make a family.
Still sewing
squinting in the dim light
in room C barrack 4 block 4
she whispers
Remember
keep your underwear
in good repair
in case of accident
don't bring shame
on us.

□

THIRTY YEARS UNDER

I had packed up
my wounds in a cast
iron box
sealed it
labeled it
do not open. . .
ever. . .

and traveled blind
for thirty years

until one day I heard
a black man with huge bulbous eyes
say
there is nothing more
humiliating
more than beatings
more than curses
than being spat on

like a dog.

☐

CINCINNATI

Freedom at last
in this town aimless
I walked against the rush
hour traffic
My first day
in a real city
where

no one knew me.

No one except one
hissing voice that said
dirty jap
warm spittle on my right cheek.
I turned and faced
the shop window
and my spittled face
spilled onto a hill
of books.
Words on display.

In Government Square
people criss-crossed
the street
like the spokes of
a giant wheel.

I lifted my right hand
but it would not obey me.

My other hand fumbled
for a hankie.

My tears would not
wash it. They stopped
and parted.
My hankie brushed
the forked
tears and spittle
together.
I edged toward the curb
loosened my fisthold
and the bleached laced
mother-ironed hankie blossomed in
the gutter atop teeth marked
gum wads and heeled candy wrappers.

Everyone knew me.

☐

III. OTHER POEMS

FREEDOM IN MANHATTAN

We were three girls
minding our distance
two thousand miles from home
crouched in darkness behind
the covered bathtub
in the kitchen.
To some boys
we weren't home
in this cold water flat
one jump from the East River.

Voices and hard knuckles
banged away on our door
Let us in, Harry sent us.

> Lock up boys for
> knocking up your door?
> roared the sergeant behind
> his desk, Come back,
> come back when ya got
> real troubles.
> Our hands clutched
> the playpen railing
> He licked the point of his
> pencil and waved it
> back and forth over our souls.

The next day
hard fists
knocked on, unhinged
and battered
our defenses.

We were three big girls
in red shoelaces
winding down the
squadcar window
looking for
Mr. Knuckles.

They drove us once
around the block then back to
one jump from the East River.
Look girls, don't make trouble.
Move out, move out, they said.
But the rent's cheap, we said.
Virgins are cheaper, they said.

☐

LOOKING OUT

It must be odd
to be a minority
he was saying.
I looked around
and didn't see any.
So I said
Yeah
it must be.

☐

TO THE LADY

The one in San Francisco who asked
Why did the Japanese Americans let
the government put them in
those camps without protest?

Come to think of it I

        should've run off to Canada
        should've hijacked a plane to Algeria
        should've pulled myself up from my
        bra straps
        and kicked'm in the groin
        should've bombed a bank
        should've tried self-immolation
        should've holed myself up in a
        woodframe house
        and let you watch me
        burn up on the six o'clock news
        should've run howling down the street
        naked and assaulted you at breakfast
        by AP wirephoto
        should've screamed bloody murder
        like Kitty Genovese

    Then

YOU would've

> come to my aid in shining armor
> laid yourself across the railroad track
> marched on Washington
> tattooed a Star of David on your arm
> written six million enraged
> letters to Congress

But we didn't draw the line
anywhere
law and order Executive Order 9066
social order moral order internal order

YOU let'm
I let'm
All are punished.

☐

HERE

I was always
a starting person
like sprouts and shoots
or a part person
like slices and slivers
which is why
neighbor boys called out
MIT SUEY CHOP SUEY

□

THERE

Once when I went back
to where I came from
I was sent to school
in clothes "Made in Japan"
and small children along
the riverbank stopped jumping
rope and sing-sang:

America no ojo-o san
doko ni iku-u
America no ojo-o san
doko ni iku-u

Girl from America
where are you going?
Girl from America
where are you going?

□

THE SPEECH

Zambia stood before the Council of Churches
a prepared text held upright
under one corner of the dashiki
covering his black naked body.
The delegates in silent hundreds
stood openly
ready and willing for the roar
to tear their flesh.

"We..."
Then for five full minutes,
Zambia, 50, wept.

☐

THE FOUNDATION

This could be the land
where everything grows.
Bulldozers had sifted up
large pieces of parched woods and
worthless rocks.
Bilateral buildings
to be are not yet.

Meanwhile on this dust
I counted seven shapes
of sturdy greys and greens
some small and slender
vertical parallels.
No one planted them here with squared T's.
Some weblike tentacles reaching out
toward rounded rotundas.

Molded by no one.

Here
starshaped with tiny speckles,
are these the intruders in my garden
of new seedlings?
My garden carefully fed and fettered?
Of course.
I pronounced their execution
with a pinch of my fingers.

But here
among myriad friends
they flourish in weedy wilderness,
boldly gracing several acres
of untended land.
Tomorrow they shall be banished from their home.

And watered by many droplets
of human sweat
will sprout another college
where
disciplined minds finely honed
will grow
in carefully
planted rows.

No room for random weeds.

☐

LIFELINE

My tent is shrinking
I crawl about the ground floor
in
a death cycle

look up
and see
stitches of light.
I yearn to push out
my mouth
and reach
for deep breath.
I hear
the man
with the
bicycle pump
and
fumbling
fingers
not
feeling
his way in.

Don't you see
I hiss
the arrows at the top
narrow
to one
witness.
But he stood at my tomb
holding the tube like a corsage.

☐

A LIFE STORY

Many people do stick it out for a while
in dust free germ free people free room
in the hospital said the family doctor.
I opted for semi-lethal free smog and
daily treatments at the respiration center,
took up sculpting at Nishan Toor's studio,
made a dozen busts,
and drove myself to teaching English.

My creative energies included growing
a uterine tumor even
but the gynecologist said he would not
operate unless a lung man stood by
in case of malfunction of my upper parts
while he was into my lower parts.
The lung man then took more X-rays and more
tests and declared:
    Looks like
    usual asthma to me.

After seven years of being out of practice
living with the notion of not dying
took some getting used to
but then most of the time now
we can live with it.

☐

MODELS

Rows of white flags
in the rain
fluttered a livid invitation
to open houses.
Eyes unblinking watched us
march gently
into the underseas
drowned town
where blue fallopian lamps
lit the cement walls.
We arrived in hard skulls
and entered a skeletal sconce
which became our home.
Now we live here
willingly.

☐

IN SANTA CRUZ

Pliable pines
following earth's bent
leaned towards winds
past and gone.

I heard words of passersby
Look
Those trees
How natural!

Under these shades
making rhythmic
directional arrows
my young child tumbled
loped
strained against
steel supports.
Fell.

Here you go
my wind up doll
on your pins,
I said.
Metallic music.
Look Mother,
I can almost touch.

Home again
my tool snapped away
wires crippling
a Christmas gift:
my bonsai.

☐

WELFARE ISLAND

for Rose

There's our prize
patient old abbie envied by all
in ward D for her loving
sons daughters cousins
who come in
turns a clockwork parade
arms outstretched bringing
things   kisses   one-minute games.

Three mercurial grandchildren today
see how she charades for them
their little family butterfly
with no voice.
Watch now
abbie makes a sign with two fingers.

They play:
Penny's poodle had two puppies, grandma?
Sammy's cut his second tooth?
No?
No dummies
grandma's making a V, not two
Jack's team won today?
Yes, see, she nods, I'm right.

There they go
they bounce and troop out
everyday the same
different people and there abbie sits
happy and enclosed in her
metal framed bed all eyes
watch.
Now ward D will sleep
with no memories
but listen
that slow moaning
from the throat with no voice.

Abbie
are you okay?
Shall I call a doctor?

☐

SILVER ANNIVERSARY

On the surface you hardly noticed
a ripple
you never suspected that
with every stroke, so much
seaweed
would drip from your fingertips.

I have been busy
these last twenty-five years
feeding barnacles
with sharp teeth,
filling castaway bottles,
greening rocks
and covering your undersides
with chains of nippled beads
and warm moss.

If you put me out to dry
my verdant handwriting
will stretch wide across
the beach.
I will crunch beneath
you at every step
and then
when the tide turns
I will come alive in the water
like an involuted Japanese flower.

At night we work
to loosen our tangled limbs
leave trails of
phosphorescent sparks.

□

ANOTHER MODEL

I did a reading with the women
in the Watts poetry group
and they said
We aren't into this women's lib thing
because we are still developing.
I talked with a Third World woman
at the International Women's Conference
and she said
I'm not into this women's lib thing
because I am still helping
our men
who are still developing.

I say
in my small frame
are two super developed cultures
but look
where I am!

☐

PUNCH BAG

I flaunted the spectre
of my liberation
and Yosh said
A good insurance policy
in widowhood you will do well.

☐

MIRROR MIRROR

People keep asking where I come from
says my son.
Trouble is   I'm american on the inside
                and oriental on the outside

    No Kai
    Turn that outside in
    THIS is what American looks like.

☐

Desert Run
Poems and Stories

*For my brothers
Mike, Tosh, and Joe*

ACKNOWLEDGMENTS

I would like to thank Sarie Munemitsu Hylkema of the Multi-cultural Women Writers for being a patient sounding board during the evolution of some of these pieces and Dr. Katharine Newman, founder of MELUS, Multi-ethnic Literature of the United States, for her meticulous reading of my manuscript and her forthright and invaluable comments.

I would like to thank Nellie Wong, Merle Woo and the late Karen Brodine for their strength of spirit in their political activism providing a creative impulse for some of these poems; Flo McAlary for opening up the desert world to me; and Peggy Boegeman for her continuous encouragement as well as prodigious work with the Humanities Council making ethnic writings, including my poems, more accessible to students throughout the country. I would like to thank Allie Light and Irving Saraf for filming a version of "I Learned to Sew" in "Mitsuye and Nellie'" before I recognized its potential.

I would like to thank those Asian American writers who walked the lonely path before me and others who continue to write against all odds: Sui Sin Far, Toshio Mori, Hisaye Yamamoto, Monica Sone, Maxine Hong Kingston, Janice Mirikitani and many others.

I would like to thank my mother, Hide Yasutake, and my mother-in-law, Nabe Iha, for their inspired lives; and finally, my husband, Yoshikazu, and our children and grandchildren (Jeni and Phil, Stephen and Sharon, Kai and Hedi, Aaron and Jason) for making our dreams for the future possible.

TABLE OF CONTENTS

I. WHERE I STAY

DESERT RUN

□

I return to the desert
where criminals
were abandoned to wander
away to their deaths
where scorpions
spiders
snakes
lizards
and rats
live in outcast harmony
where the sculptor's wreck
was reclaimed
by the gentle drifting sands.

We approach the dunes while
the insistent flies bother our ears
the sound of crunching gravel under
our shoes cracks the desolate stillness
and opens our way.

Everything is done in silence here:
the wind fingers fluted stripes
over mounds and mounds of sand
the swinging grasses sweep
patterns on the slopes
the sidewinder passes out of sight.
I was too young to hear silence before.

II.

I spent 547 sulking days here
in my own dreams
there was not much to marvel at
I thought
only miles of sagebrush and
lifeless sand.

I watched the most beautiful
sunsets in the world and saw nothing
forty years ago
I wrote my will here
my fingers moved slowly in the
hot sand the texture of whole wheat flour
three words: I died here
the winds filed them away.

I am back to claim my body
my carcass lies
between the spiny branches
of two creosote bushes
it looks strangely like a small calf
left to graze and die
half of its bones are gone
after all these years

but no matter
I am satisfied
I take a dry stick
and give myself
a ritual burial.

III.

Like the bull snakes brought
into this desert by the soldiers
we were transported here
to drive away rattlers
in your nightmares
we were part of some one's plan
to spirit away spies
in your peripheral vision.

My skin turned pink brown
in the bright desert light
I slithered in the matching sand
doing what you put me here to do
we were predators at your service.
I put your mind at ease.

I am that odd creature.
the female bull snake
I flick my tongue in your face
an image trapped in your mirror.
You will use me or
you will honor me in a shrine
to keep me pure.

IV.

At night the outerstellar darkness
above is only an arm's length away
I am pressed by the silence around me
the stars are bold as big as quarters
against the velvet blue sky
their beams search for the marrow
of my bones
I shiver as I stumble my way to
the outhouse.

In the morning we find
kangaroo rats
have built mounds of messy homes
out of dry sticks and leavings
behind our wagon
They have accepted our alien presence.
The night creatures keep a discreet
distance.

V.

The desert is the lungs of the world.
This land of sudden lizards and nappy ants
is only useful when not used
We must leave before we feel we can
change it.

When we leave the dirt roads
my body is thankful for the
paved ride the rest of the way
home.
Rows of yucca trees with spiked crowns
wave stiffly at us
Some watch us arms akimbo.

I cannot stay in the desert
where you will have me nor
will I be brought back in a cage
to grace your need for exotica.
I write these words at night
for I am still a night creature
but I will not keep a discreet distance.

If you must fit me to your needs
I will die
and so will you.

山田えツエ

HOLE IN THE WALL

☐

I understood why Geronimo
had fought for so long to hold
the land he loved.

Agnes Smedley,
Daughter of Earth

We bumble into the Mojave
our narrowed lives still
clinging to our skins
the watching sun shrinks
the pupils of our eyes
the grey desert enters
through our contracting lids

I am not afraid of the recoiling
sun when night elbows in
without sign
we build a fire
open our mouths to feed
our tastebuds for a truce that
pulses in the darkness.

We awaken with the sun
impatient to shed our citiness.

山田ミツヱ

LICHENS
☐

While we sleep in our tents
tightly zipped in
and together
new generations of
lichens spill over
on sandblasted rocks
like orange marmalade
storm-bearing westerlies
whip fireflies
flitting outside
our thin nylon walls.

Between the
host culture and us.
there is only time
and patience for
lichens slowly release
corroding chemicals
on resisting floors.

Volcanic mass turns to soil
one grain at a time
enough for pioneering moss
and fledgling ferns to
make our desert lawn.

山田ミツエ

DESERT UNDER GLASS

□

Nobody sees a flower —
really —
it is so small —
we haven't the time —
and to see takes time —
like to have a friend takes time.

Georgia O'Keefe

Look at the buckwheat
magnified
the biologist
coaxes my myopic eye
over glass
a dusty round desert flower
with a humble household name
blooms
a cluster of brilliant
orchid-like shapes and colors
the buckwheat
growing on a crust
of unmasked earth
can be seen
by one
steady
inward
eye.

CACTI

□

I am an expectant guest
waiting to be surprised
but my hosts refuse my demands;
they stand mute before me.
Armed with a desert Baedeker
I wait.
I read that the barrel cacti's
accordion skins expand
for water storage
after storms
and contract with use
through the year.
The cacti take
a hundred years to mature.
I want to see it for myself.

Friends and aging take time.
The jumping cholla flays
its quilled armor at me
and dare me to come close.
I have too little time
to spare for
I am only one of the ephemerals.

The desiccating sun forces
her way over me and
preserves me into the dust.
My desert never ages
it is already old.

山田ミツエ

DESERT MYSTIQUE
□

*There was a line of shallow graves; they used
to count on dropping a man or two of every new
gang of coolies brought out in the hot sun.*

Mary Austin,
The Land of Little Rain

I.

Every year on the face of glossy
Christmas cards strange wise men
robed and jeweled cross
the desert on camels
with no footprints
guided by one tailed
meteor smoldering
in the sky.

Every year I come here
bearing private gifts
to walk under a million stars
between giant yuccas
looming everywhere.
Their roots spread
wide on the surface
expecting
drops
of my blood.

II.

I am transfused
by the creosote
shrubs squatting
close to the ground
by their vibrant wax leaves
not parched
never wilted
by their windmill petals
flourishing yellow ocher
in season
their roots claw
deep under for
cool water
evenly spaced
on this wide expanse of land.

Among these short shrubs
stand the mesquites with
deciduous leaves
faded shades of saffron
blossom on crooked branches
Their roots meet
my creosotes and finally
join hands
at seven feet under
like the genetic code of Asian
ancestral ties
the temperature underground
is constant.

In the haze of night
I look for my creosotes
growing in patterned rows
around a natural boulder
like a well-combed
Zen garden.

山田ミツエ

II. RETURNING

AMERICAN SON

☐

When I was ten
I rolled my hair in rags
for Shirley Temple ringlets
polished my teeth white
for a Pepsodent smile
clattered about in slick
tap shoes
so my father
sent me away
to his mother in Japan
who took me in
because I was hers,

a piece of an only son sent
home like dirty laundry to be
washed and pressed
then returned to America less
tomboy American more
ladylike Japanese

a daily reminder of him
who only yesterday
crossed that river
on a swinging narrow bridge
to school

a thin-boned body like his
that worked years ago
in the teeming rice fields
until dark.

Satokaeri
returning
to one's origins
wherever that may be
a tradition in Japan
caring for grandmothers
and great grandmothers
my father said
do this
for me.

Satokaeri
returning
and turning
for an absentee son
whose memories of boyhood
days hardened like
frosting on an uneaten cake.

I came unformed
took sliding runs on polished corridors
never closed *shojis* behind me
never stopped asking
questions
about Grandmother's curly hair
she unrolled daily and ironed
straight with a rod
warmed on coals,
never stopped being frightened
by Great Grandmother's smile
showing black teeth
she dyed with a wad of cotton
dipped in berry juice
like the *grande dames*
in old Japanese movies.

My grandmother answered
only questions I never asked
"Yes, your papa is my son
Yes, my landlord my son
comes home only twice
in twenty three years
once to build this house.
He was a good son.
What good
is a son
in America?"

山
田
ミ
ツ
エ

GUILTY ON BOTH COUNTS

□

I glide in by Bullet Train
to my birthplace in Kyushu
after forty years
only the elevated tracks
that dwarf the village scene
jangle my framed memory.

I am greeted by my cousin
the country doctor
"Ma yoku kite kureta."
So good of you to come.
Her new clinic overlooks
a sculpted pond stocked
with fifty active koi
flashing in the sun.
Nurses shuffle about
in quick steps
along the outer corridors

while I
the honored guest
am left alone talking
with Kiichan
the family mina bird
perched at the hallway entrance
babbling in Japanese
*"Moshi moshi, moshi moshi
gomen nasai, gomen nasai."*
"Kiichan, try some English.
Hello hello, excuse me excuse me."

A human voice
interrupts us
"Moshi moshi
gomen nasai."
Standing at the threshhold
is a picture of a woman
in a stiff kimono top and pants:
the brim of her straw hat
tied close to her head
with a blue and white towel
balanced on one hip
a flat bamboo basket
heavy with slender Japanese egg plants
giant cucumbers in alternate spokes
in the middle a small round watermelon.

Here is real local color
a rare sight in modern Japan.
I want to run for my camera
but the picture speaks
"Gomen nasai isogashii toko..."
Excuse me I'm sorry to bother you but...
I muster up my best American Japanese
"Iiye sonna koto ari masen"
Oh no, not at all
she places the basket at my feet
"Dozo, kore Sensei ni..."
Please, this is for the doctor.

She hesitates
her mouth a tight-lipped polite smile
aware of my grinning rudeness
I descend to my knees
"Arigatoh gozai masu."
Thank you very much.
I practice my best bow
"Arigatoh gozai masu."
I trot out my kin credentials
to accept her gift.
"You see, I am the doctor's cousin
visiting from America."

My cousin's voice
a soft drumroll
drops between us.
"Mah
how beautiful
Arigatoh
Shiro-san
you are
always
so generous."
but the gift bearer's eyes
smash through our ceremonies.
She is gone.

"Yurushite yatte?"
Will you forgive her?
This is August
She is from Hiroshima
"Tondemo nai koto dakedo..."
This is outrageous but
you see...
her whole family...
I stop her with a wave of my hand.

I understand I say
"America demo..."
In America too
many people blame
me, you
for Pearl Harbor

She is wide-eyed.
"Nani? America demo. . ?"
What? In America too. . ?
She touches her nose
with her forefinger
a gesture I remember from childhood.
"Sonna koto watashiga..?"
They think I..?
I would do such a thing?
I tap my own nose facing her
"Hai, watashimo."
Yes, and me.

The Bullet Train whirs past
on elevated tracks
over miles of plush green rice fields
nine hours from Tokyo.

OBON: FESTIVAL OF THE DEAD
☐

On the day of the festival Uncle leads our
procession snapping his kimono sleeves as he swings
his arms. My cousins and I carry fresh-smelling
wooden buckets filled with garden flowers over our
arms like picnic baskets. Uncle's new wife motions to me
with the broom and rake in both hands, hurrying me
along as I lag behind on new wooden *getas*.

At the gravesite together we scrub the family
headstone, weed, sweep and rake the ground around
under Aunty's firm command and Cousin Fumiko
whispers in my ear she is not my real mother, my
real *Okaasan* is here, we are taking her home today.

I watch the only Aunty I know who is arranging
masses of flowers about the grave in slow motion
until Uncle in quaint country dialect barks *"Sorede
yoka."* That's enough. He kneels at the grave
and in formal language reserved only, I
suppose, for deceased wives says *"Omukae ni
kimashita, sa-a sa-a ikimasho."* We have come to
take you home. Come, come, let us go.

I am told to cup my hands behind by back to carry
Obasan home. At nine I feel too old for childish
games but I play anyway. I am the only child here.
In America her name will be read on Sunday during
Prayers for the Dead but over here I am trying to
balance the spirit of *Obasan* on my back
clattering over pebbled roads back to the village.

We entertain *Obasan* royally all day on this sweltering August day. Aunty has prepared her rival's favorite dishes: *udon*, steaming hot noodles in clear soup; *imo*, sweet potatoes baked on hot charcoals; and *omanju*, sweet dumplings. Her place is set with chopsticks on the left side. Uncle says she was a *"wagamama no onna,"* a self-centered woman, but my Cousin Fumiko shakes her head, her eyes glistening and says, "She was only left-handed." I make a note of this in my mind to tell my left-handed brother back home in America "Believe it or not way over there in Japan we had one maverick aunty who used chopsticks with her left hand too!"

After dinner we take *Obasan's* treasured silk *kimonos* out of tissue papers. We girls are transformed into singing, dancing maidens. Cousin Fumiko teaches us *Obasan's* favorite songs and dances. We make a place for her and play her favorite games. When she loses, my cousin whines just like her late mother, *"Kuyashii, kuyashii,"* I hate it, I hate it. Aunty and I, strangers together, have come to know the real *Obasan* on this day, *Obon*, Festival of the Dead.

At dusk we carry *Obasan* on a handcrafted boat to
the beach and join a hundred other villagers with
their own dead. The priests in tall hats and white
robes standing knee-deep in water chant their
blessings over our vessels. *Obasan's* boat lists
and sways in the water from the weight of too many
omanju we had loaded for her long journey back to
her place of rest. Uncle lights the torch on the
bow and pushes her out as he coaxes *"Ike, ike,"* Go
on, go on. Her sharp bow cuts the water as she
joins the shoal of lights out to sea.

My cousins call out *"Sayonara Okaasan mata rainen
ni neh?"* Goodbye Mother until next year? Aunty dabs
her eyes with her handkerchief says, *"Anta shiawase
da neh?"* Aren't you lucky? I nod in confusion. The
sky is aflame as thousands of silent Roman
candles float out with the tide.

山田ミツエ

RETURNING

□

The voice blaring through the loudspeaker seemed to be announcing that they were about to enter a tunnel, which it pronounced *tone-neru.* She was able to understand only bits and pieces of the rapid-fire Japanese. In a second, the Shinkansen train plunged into the tunnel with a loud whirr and the lights in the car flashed on.

"This is the longest underwater tunnel in the..."

Emiko was not sure what the next words were. In Japan? In the East? In the world? She took a closer look at the map. They must have left the island of Honshu and were now in the tunnel connecting it to Kyushu. She was amazed to see the distance they had covered: 731 miles from Tokyo to Fukuoka, the northern gateway to the island of Kyushu. The voice continued in breathless spurts: *"tone-neru...*great feat...*tone-neru*...miracle...*tone-neru*...proud moment...*tone-neru*... *tone-neru...*" When her last travel "companions," two well-behaved school girls, got off the train at the last stop, Emiko took out her English tourist guidebook. Perhaps she should have taken it out earlier as a conversation gambit. It might have made her feel less like an invisible fixture in the third seat as they rattled away in Japanese. But, she reminded herself, she was trying to "pass" for a native Japanese and had not wanted to give herself away. After all, she couldn't have it both ways.

Emiko put the map away and turned to look out the window, already forgetting that they were now in the underwater *tone-neru.* Instead of the sight of duplicate scores of apartment houses with an array of colorful *futons* draped over the terrace railings, or patches of signs with Japanese characters dotting the landscape, she saw her own reflection in the dark glass. She looked remarkably "well-preserved" for a woman her age, as her children might have said. She had had her hair cut short so that the grey around her temples would be not quite as conspicuous. Her sleeveless, white knit dress remained unwrinkled in spite of the six hours of restless squirming in her seat. The dress was a good choice, one among several plain white or off-white outfits she had bought hastily a few days before her departure when her mother had suggested that middle-aged Japanese women simply do not wear bright summer prints as the American women do in California.

Neither do they travel around by themselves, Emiko thought, remembering all the discussion in Tokyo among her male cousins about who should accompany her to Kyushu. She had stood firm; in

America, she lied, she traveled around by herself all the time. She must, she hoped she sounded convincing, pay her respects to her aunt in Fukuoka for her father's sake. Since his death, they had not kept in touch with his family, and she really should go by herself. Her cousins finally agreed with her and retreated gracefully, not wanting to impose. The week in Tokyo with her mother's relatives was a pleasant transition for her. They enjoyed an easy camaraderie, the older ones recalling her earlier visit, and the younger ones politely chuckling over her outmoded Japanese expressions and helping her, at her urging, to update her language. Her expressions were from the *Meiji jidai,* her mother's generation, they told her. Remember to ask for the *otearai* when she wants to go to the restroom. It literally means "the place one washes one's hands," or even *toire* for toilet will do, but never the vulgar term, *benjo.* And never refer to the friendly uniformed officer on the street as *junsa.* The new expression is *omawarisan,* "the person who walks around." *Junsa* only refers to policemen who deal with criminals.

This figure in the mirror sitting primly in the straight-backed train seat could be her mother, Emiko thought. She wished that she felt as cool and unruffled as this woman in her white knit dress. Now that she was really on her own, she missed her cousins in Tokyo who might have helped her in her search.

Who would have thought that only two weeks ago this trip was to have been something quite different, a Silver Anniversary present Emiko and Yukio were going to give themselves? When he announced ten days before their scheduled departure that because of an emergency situation at work it would be impossible for him to leave at this time, her immediate reaction was anger. She wanted to cancel the whole trip.

"Why not take your mother along?" Yukio had suggested, trying to temporize.

Well, perhaps. Her mother had not been back to visit her family since the end of "the war." But much to Emiko's surprise, instead of jumping at the opportunity for a free trip, her mother demurred. No, she must not; she had too much to do. She was in charge of the food at her church festival the following weekend.

Well then, why not? Why not a first time solo trip, Emiko thought. She had never in her life gone on a long trip anywhere alone, without a parent, her older brother, or her husband and children.

The following morning after Emiko made her decision, her mother dropped by for a cup of coffee and talked nostalgically about her own childhood as if nostalgia were something that could be transferred.

"This is your *satokaeri,* Emiko," she had said.

"Well, it's more like returning to *your* origins rather than mine. Are you sure you won't change your mind about going with me?" Emiko tried again.

"No, I cannot. At least not as long as *Otama-san* is living there," she said evenly.

"Who?"

"*Anno onna*, " Emiko's mother said under her breath.

Anno onna? That woman! So that was it. Emiko was stunned. How long has it been since she had thought about the person she only knew at one time as *anno onna*? It never occurred to her that the woman might have had a name. During Emiko's childhood, *anno onna* came to her in the dark of the night through closed doors. Her parents only quarreled in muffled voices in their bedroom at night after they thought the children were asleep. Whatever else they quarreled about, Emiko never knew, only that the words *anno onna* would come shooting through the wall from their bedroom to hers between murmurs.

"You might try looking her up while you're there," her mother said without conviction.

"What on earth for?" Emiko exclaimed in English, the language she always resorted to for spontaneous outbursts. She was thoroughly mystified.

"You always wanted a younger sister ever since you were a little girl. Don't you remember that?"

"Yes, of course I do. So, what about it?" Emiko was beginning to feel a vague uneasiness.

Her mother looked down at her hands clasped tightly on her lap, and said, "*Moshika shitara*, you have a younger sister in Japan."

"What do you mean, *moshika shitara?* How could I 'maybe' have a sister?"

Emiko's mother sat bolt upright in her chair, as if in a formal inquisition. She had obviously been thinking of this moment for some time and was prepared for the shock her announcement would cause in her daughter. It was this dignity and this outward calm that Emiko admired about her mother, except at moments like these. They sat with their elbows resting on the kitchen table as they fingered their empty coffee cups. A dog barked somewhere in the distance. A plane from the nearby airport roared overhead. An impatient driver was gunning past the house. Emiko remembered seeing *that woman* only once, for a few seconds, during her childhood, an image that had become indelibly etched in her mind.

It was one of those Saturday afternoons. Emiko's mother often visited with her friend, Mrs. Nomura, who operated the *Furoba*, a community bath in the Japanese section of downtown Seattle. Emiko and her brother, Teru, must have been five and six years old respectively. Their father would always drop them off on his way to his regular club meetings at a nearby Japanese restaurant and pick them up later. That afternoon, because their father was unusually late in picking them up, Emiko's mother told Mrs. Nomura that they had better take a taxi home because the children were getting restless. Emiko and Teru, excited by this novel treat, clambered into the backseat of the cab and propped themselves up on their knees to look out the rear window. They drove through the center of town and across the bridge. Their house was one of the older houses overlooking the bay. When they were a few blocks from their house, the children thought they saw their father's car behind them and shouted in unison, "There's Papa!"

Papa's car was a bright blue Buick with red wheels which they could always spot from blocks away. Their mother had to call out "sutoppu, sutoppu" several times before the cab driver understood that she was telling him to stop. The blue Buick had caught up with them as the cab pulled over to the side. Both children leaned out the window and shouted, "Papa, Papa!"

Emiko only saw a glimpse of her who was sitting on the passenger side of the front seat, her mother's place. The woman raised her hand, but instead of waving as Emiko thought she was going to do, she pulled her black hat over her face and plumped down out of sight. It all happened in a few seconds as the car sped past them, but the woman's face in pasty white makeup with bright red lipstick that shaped her mouth to a small round "O" was so distinctive that Emiko never forgot her. At once their mother was out of the cab on the street side and looked as if she were about to run after Papa's departing car. The children were standing behind her in the middle of the street. Emiko's mother recovered her composure in an instant, paid the cab driver and started walking down the middle of the street toward their home. Emiko couldn't remember exactly what her mother was wearing, but her handsome figure, dressed in the fashionable western dress of the 30's, was recorded so repeatedly for their family album that Emiko could picture what her mother must have looked like on that day, leading the procession down the street, her two children skipping along behind her single file. The children were in a carefree mood for here was their mother, always a stickler for rules and regulations, giving them full permission to break one of her own safety rules. When they reached their house they saw that their father's car was not parked in front, but the children knew enough to keep silent.

Later that night, Emiko was awakened by her mother's unusually high-pitched voice. She could hear the words *anno onna* punctuating each utterance. The white face of the passenger in her father's car now became one with the phrase *anno onna* in her mind.

Slowly, in Japanese, sometimes in halting broken English, her mother spoke. After Papa died twenty years ago, she said, she had a safecracker open his personal safe in their bedroom closet. She had never thought much about what he kept in that safe through all those years. She had assumed they were *daiji na mono*, important papers, that wives need not concern themselves with. She had never known the combination to the safe, was never curious enough to ask about it. When the safe was finally opened, she found letters. Nothing but letters. That was all. They were in small bundles, each tied neatly, deliberately, with pieces of white cotton string, letters from Japan dating back more than a dozen years. A few of them were in *katakana* in a childish scrawl. These were short letters of one or two lines.

Emiko's mother closed her eyes and seemed to be reciting from memory, "*Onatsukashii Oto-o sama*, My beloved father, Thank you for the money. *Okaa-san* and I are well. Aiko."

The rest of the letters were in a woman's fluid script, an educated hand, she said. She tried to read a few of them but her mind was in a turmoil. She could not see the words very well. She cupped her hands together on the table to show Emiko the size of the bundles.

"*Akirete shimatta.* I was astonished. There were so many," she said, "letters all tied up carefully into bundles. Under the bundles was a *shorui* of some kind in English."

"Where are the letters and that document now, Mother?" By this time Emiko was leaning halfway over the table as if she were hard of hearing and needed to get closer.

"*Sorega neh*, that's just it," her mother said with a deep sigh, "*Ai-chan ni taishite tondemonai kotoshita.* For *Ai-chan*, it was a terrible thing that I did."

"Tell me, Mother, where are the letters now?"

"*Neh, Do-o shimasho*, Emiko. What shall I do, Emiko? I did a very bad thing. I...," Emiko's mother, who had been stoical throughout her story until then was unable to continue. She held the imaginary bundles in her hands and made a tossing motion toward the floor.

"I threw them in the fireplace. They were all..." she could not bring herself to say the word "burned." They both sat looking at the spot on the floor, as if together they were watching the letters slowly burn in the fireplace.

It was Emiko who broke the painful silence.

"But the document under the letters? Did you save it at least?"

"*Ai-chan* was probably around seven when she wrote those letters. About nineteen or twenty when your father died."

No, I suppose she did not, Emiko decided. She noticed that her mother was referring to Aiko by her affectionate name, *Ai-chan*, as if the child had been part of her for some time, keeping track of her age through the years, like a mother who had "lost" a child.

"*Sumanai kotoshita*, Emiko, but that was only two days after Papa passed away, the day I found those letters."

Sumanai kotoshita, tondemonai kotoshita. I did an unforgivable thing, a terrible thing. Her mother had obviously reproached herself with these words many times through the years. But Papa? What would he have thought? Emiko remembered their earnest father/daughter talks. They had become close during those last few years before his death. After she and Yukio were married, Emiko had become more than ever sensitive to the tension between her parents and appointed herself their marriage counselor. She found it easier to talk to her father who was fluent in English.

"Maybe you need to try making up with her," Emiko would tell him. "Why don't you take her out sometime?"

They only discussed his "affairs" in general terms. He could not understand why her mother felt so neglected. Look how much better off she was compared to most Issei wives, he would say. A nice house, nice clothes. So maybe he slipped once or twice, but that's the way it was with most Japanese men. Then he would try to make her laugh by gesturing with his hands in a playful manner and say, "Don't you see, Emiko, it's sort of an accepted Japanese custom."

"Emiko, you do understand, don't you," her mother was pleading, "why I did what I did? His lawyer was going to come to look through his papers the next day. I didn't want him to find those letters."

"After all," Papa used to say, "what I did was *not* unforgivable, but your mother is a very unforgiving person."

"Please try to understand, Emiko," her mother continued, "I was too ashamed for him, for you and for Teru."

On one occasion when they were discussing "the subject" again, Papa looked at her with an air of helplessness and exclaimed, "Good god, how long does a man have to pay?"

Because she needed to talk to someone of her failure as a marriage counselor, Emiko called Teru and confided, "Poor Papa, he is such a little boy. He actually thinks *he's* the one who's paying."

"You now have a husband and children of your own, Emiko. You *do* understand how I felt then, don't you?" her mother was saying.

Emiko looked at her memory of Papa, her flamboyant, lovable Papa whom she thought she knew so well. Those years when she and Papa were having those "counseling" sessions were the very years he must have been exchanging letters with Aiko and her mother, making plans for them.

Emiko's mother had had twenty years rehearsing her lines but Emiko was still processing the information in her mind. Aiko! She had a sister less than ten years younger than she. Was the document a birth certificate? Perhaps an application for entry to the United States? Or an application to a college? Aiko. What hopes and dreams of hers vanished twenty years ago when their father died? Where could she be now?

Emiko slid her body around the table to her mother's side, pressed her hand gently on her shoulder and asked, "Mother, did you at least let them know when Papa died?"

Her mother gave her a pained look and shook her head.

"How could I? I didn't have the address."

"Didn't any letters come after he died?"

"No. There must have been an intermediary, probably a close friend."

Emiko cast about in her mind for names of her father's close friends and remembered two who were still around, but discarded the notion of contacting them.

"There still might be another copy of the application with their address on it among Papa's papers! Didn't we keep some of them?"

Emiko's mother continued to shake her head. No, he was a very careful person. A good businessman. He was very orderly about important matters. She said that when she realized what she had done, she even asked some of her friends a few months after the funeral if they knew anything about this woman. She grimaced, remembering that her friends had only gossip to offer but no information.

"The letters were simply signed 'Tamaye.' I knew. I knew about her."

As if she needed to acknowledge something she had been denying to herself through all these years, she repeated again, "I knew about her and your father. I knew when she was working at the restaurant in

Seattle. But then about a year before the war, I heard she went back to Japan, and I thought it was over."

"Mother, do you think Papa's sister in Fukuoka would know?"

"I didn't read any of the letters. I was too upset. But her penmanship was perfect. She was only a waitress at that restaurant, but I could tell by her script that she must have been very learned. He saved all of her letters through all those years."

Obasan in Fukuoka. She was the only surviving family member on Papa's side.

"That woman was fortunate," her mother was saying. "She was a very fortunate person."

The Shinkansen train had suddenly roared out of the tunnel. Emiko involuntarily closed her eyes against the sudden burst of light from the window. Here they were, on the Island of Kyushu. The scenery out of the window appeared to be getting progressively greener, airier, but everywhere there were still apartment buildings with the countless windows.

Satokaeri. Returning. It was exactly forty years since her first visit to Japan when she was eight years old. She and Teru accompanied their mother to visit her large family in Tokyo. It seemed to them at the time that the trip was no different from their other family excursions to Mexico and Canada, except that their father was not able to go with them, Emiko now remembered. (For business reasons, he had said, and then he went alone a few months later to visit with his aging parents.) On that trip, Emiko felt and acted like any other foreign tourist in a strange land, but she was to discover later that the one trip to Japan had a kind of staying power that all other vacation trips to new places did not.

After returning home she believed she understood why non-Japanese Americans so often referred to her "cultural heritage" as if it were something tangible, like a family heirloom that was passed on to her by her parents. Sometimes she accepted this notion because it was convenient when she wanted to reject her heritage. Concrete "things" were easier to reject than abstract ideas. On the other hand, she never really examined her parents' often expressed belief that her legacy was an illusive heritage that resided somewhere "over there." Returning. Perhaps she must now come to claim whatever it was she had missed before. Modern Tokyo felt too much like being back home. The rural parts of Fukuoka would be closer to that origin her mother insisted she was returning to.

Hakata in Fukuoka City was the end of the line on the Shinkansen train. When Emiko stepped out of her car, the first sight that greeted her was a brigade of six women in white uniforms, their heads wrapped in white towels, standing conspicuously on the platform. Each carried a plastic bucket and a broom. She was momentarily distracted by them for they were an unusual sight, women in their forties and fifties in the work force. She wondered if they were single independent women or working wives. Would they consider her rude if she were to speak to them? She had embarrassed an older woman who was shining shoes sitting on the sidewalk in Tokyo because she had stopped to ask permission to take her picture.

"*Doshite, konna mittomonai hotono...?* Why do you want a picture of such an unpresentable person?" she had said.

Her cousin who was with her tugged at her sleeves.

"It was embarrassing," her cousin laughingly told his family that evening at the dinner table. Referring to her as *Americano onna* he said, "You never know what this American woman will do next." She shuddered at the reference. Remembering that incident, he had warned her at the train station when he saw her off not to "make a spectacle" of herself in Fukuoka. She decided not to speak to the cleaning women at the station.

She hopped into one of the cabs in front of the station feeling alone and vulnerable as she asked the cab driver if he would recommend a hotel in the middle of the city. The tiny hotel room in the modest hotel he drove her to was equipped with a small refrigerator stocked with light refreshments, soft drinks, and wine. She was delighted to see a small Japanese type bathtub and felt her bones aching for a hot bath after the long train ride.

The following morning Emiko called her aunt from her hotel room.

"I'm sorry I can't come to fetch you, *Emi-chan*. Will you take a cab? You shouldn't have any trouble finding us. We live in the same place." Emiko hung up the phone and chuckled with relief. To *Obasan* it could have been only last summer instead of forty summers ago when Emiko had spent a week by herself with her paternal grandparents. No one told her exactly why she was left there alone with them while her mother and Teru returned to Tokyo, but she had a sense that she was "on loan" to her grandparents to atone for her father's absence.

The cab driver pulled up in front of two weather-worn stone pillars. Emiko remembered the narrow walkway hemmed in on both sides by tall evergreens. When she found herself standing in front of an old house, much smaller than she had remembered it and now somewhat run-down, she hesitated. Should she knock on the outside or walk in and call as she has seen done in the Japanese movies? Somehow, walking straight in seemed a little friendlier, since she was expected. She opened the sliding door and called out, "*Konnichiwa.*"

In a second an older woman neatly dressed in a cool summer *yukata* appeared and exclaimed with genuine warmth, "*Ma-a, Emi-chan!* You're really here? I've waited so long! You haven't changed a bit."

"*Obasan,* it's *you* who haven't changed!" Emiko laughed.

Her aunt was sixteen years younger than her father. Emiko was quickly calculating. She was indeed a very youthful looking almost-seventy year old Japanese woman! Her aunt apologized extensively for her inability to be more hospitable. How long will Emiko stay in Kyushu? What does she plan to do while here? Where would she like to visit? Emiko saw her chance.

"*Jitsuwa,* the fact is," she said cautiously at first but quickly blurted out, "I am looking for an old friend of Papa's, a Tamaye-san. I don't remember her last name."

"*Oh, soh.* But your father's been dead for twenty years now. Why do you want to find her?"

"I have important reasons."

Obasan nodded her head thoughtfully, saying nothing. Then she abruptly excused herself and left the room. Emiko felt hopeful for the first time since hearing the story from her mother. When her aunt returned, she was carrying a shoe box size wooden box tied with a silk purple cord. The box was filled with envelopes with printed stamps on them, the kind one might buy at the post office.

"Your father wrote such beautiful letters, you know that, don't you *Emi-chan*? There was an envelope in one of these that was addressed to Kato Tamaye in Beppu." She shuffled through the envelopes and handed Emiko one that was postmarked SEATTLE, WASH. SEPT. 15, 11:30 AM, 1941. Emiko's heart jumped when she recognized her father's handwriting. Inside was a slender, Japanese-made brown envelope with the name and address written in Japanese characters.

"Is she the person you are looking for, *Emi-chan*?"

"I think so."

"Do you remember that your father came back to Japan in the fall only a few months after your trip that summer?" her aunt asked. Yes, Emiko remembered seeing a couple of rare photographs of her father and her aunt with their parents all posing proudly in quilted kimonos with white steam from the hot spring rising up behind them. Yes, that was the time, her aunt said. In fact that was the only time in years that he returned to visit them since he had left to study in America.

"Oh, your father looked so dashing. Your grandfather and grandmother were so delighted with him. He wanted to treat us all to a week at the resort hotel in Beppu. Imagine!" Her aunt's eyes sparkled as she talked.

"During the day each of us went our own way, taking hot mud baths, going for treatments to the masseuse, and shopping, because you know I loved to shop, but always we met at the inn in the later afternoon and dined together. There were a couple of nights he did not return. He explained that he'd run into some old school friends and stayed up all night talking. I didn't think much about his strange behavior until that letter came a year later," she said, pointing to the brown envelope that was in Emiko's hand.

"He asked me to deliver the letter to his friend in Beppu—in person. He was quite frantic that he had not heard from her for several months."

Emiko turned the envelope over and saw that it was sealed at the narrow end.

"I didn't know what to do," Obasan continued, tapping her chest rapidly over her heart. "I was frightened. There was talk of war everywhere. Travel was difficult although Beppu is not too far away from here. How could I take such a trip without telling my family the reason?"

"Didn't my father explain anything in his letter to you?" Emiko wondered.

"It was just like your father, you know, not to tell me anything. You see, I didn't deliver that letter. It's been in this box with the rest of his letters ever since. I didn't see any point in bringing it up when the war ended. I gather that he found her then?"

"Do you think there is a train to Beppu at this hour?" Emiko said abruptly and looked at her watch. Her aunt gasped, *"Masaka...!*Is it possible that...! Do you really think she will still be there? In Beppu? Is it that important? Your business?" Then with no further questions, her aunt went into the next room and returned in a few minutes with the information that there was indeed a train to Beppu within the hour which would arrive in Beppu City before dark.

"Your luck is with you," her aunt said, sounding very much like her mother, "there was a room available at one of the inns. I made a reservation for you. *Sa-a,* let's go outside; the cab will be here in a minute."

Obasan picked up the brown envelope that Emiko had left on the *tatami* and handed it to her niece. Did her aunt expect her to deliver it forty years late? Or was she giving it to her for the address?

Emiko did not feel up to discussing complicated matters with her in Japanese. She appreciated her aunt's discretion, a character trait she used to think was "so very Japanese" and which, in her parents or their friends, used to annoy her because it felt like indifference. She felt a deep affection for this woman who quietly and efficiently paved her way to Beppu without probing. For the first time since embarking on this trip, she felt somewhat relaxed and less driven.

The following morning Emiko was awakened by sounds of knocking. She jumped out of bed to answer the door, then realized she was in a hotel room and that the noise was from large raindrops rapping against the small windowpane. She dressed quickly and went downstairs to the lobby to hail a cab. There was only one cab available in front of the hotel, a small car that was used for tours by a private tour company.

Throughout the ride, the driver chatted incessantly and cheerfully conducting what must have been his customary tour guide routine seemingly oblivious to the pouring rain outside. Visibility was almost zero, but he pointed to the left and right, accenting his remarks with *migino ho-o* and *hidarino ho-o* and looking back occasionally to see if she were listening. Between water bursts against her window, Emiko imagined seeing trails of vapors rising out of the ground, the kind she saw in the old photograph of her father and his parents. If her mother were here, Emiko thought, she would consider all of this to be a bad omen: the sudden summer storm, the cab that wasn't a cab, and definitely this ridiculous driver. People who were out of touch with reality disrupted her mother's ordered way of thinking, and she considered them to be portents of bad luck.

When the driver stopped talking, the abrupt silence in the car startled Emiko out of her thoughts. They had stopped in front of an entrance to a house, and the storm had subsided to a slow drizzle. Whatever else Emiko pictured in her mind, it was not this beautiful modern structure that lay before her. "Are you sure this is it?" Emiko thought to herself as she paid the driver who was holding the door open for her. He thanked her and said, *"Tashikani machigai arimasen."*

There's no doubt about it. Not only was this man eccentric, he could read her mind even when she is thinking in English, she mused.

A young girl with a broom was vigorously sweeping the stepping stones that ran along the side of the house. She stopped and stared openly at Emiko, who, drawn by her eyes, directly approached her. Emiko took a deep breath. She had become aware of the heavy humidity in the air and the discomfort of her sticky clothes. No, this girl couldn't be Aiko, she thought. Aiko would be at least forty years old by now.

"Excuse me, I am sorry to disturb you, but I have come to inquire after a person by the name of Kato Tamaye-san," she addressed the girl rather stiffly and realized how silly she must have sounded, a middle-aged woman like her talking to a young person in such a formal manner. The girl seemed a little surprised, but much to Emiko's relief, responded with a faint smile and shyly asked the visitor to please step inside.

Inside the entryway was a rusty frame of an old baby carriage. This incongruous object in the impeccably kept entrance to the house gave the scene a surreal quality. Emiko was escorted into a sitting room that had the smell of fresh straw and newly finished wood, heightened by the dampness in the air; but she was still not sure if she had come to the right place. When she asked, "Does a Kato-san live here?" the girl simply said, "Just a minute please," and disappeared into the back rooms. Certainly this would not be the same house from which all those letters came more than thirty years ago. It looked too new. Could this possibly be *Otama-san's* house? *Anno Onna* with the pasty white makeup? A long wall hanging with striking bold brush strokes dominated the alcove in the spacious room. A small slender empty vase sat inobtrusively under the hanging.

Emiko heard whispering and shuffling in the side room. The sliding door opened, and there stood the girl with a large cushion under her arm. An old woman on her hands and knees appeared to be cowering behind her. The girl placed the cushion on the *tatami* floor, helped the woman situate herself on the cushion, and left without saying a word. Emiko groped about for something to say. It was always difficult for her to initiate a conversation in Japanese when there was nothing to respond to, no familiar words for her to repeat while forming new phrases in her head.

"*Kato-san desuka?* Are you Kato-san?" she ventured. The woman nodded.

Emiko introduced herself and decided to be direct, "I'm sorry to intrude into your life so suddenly after all these years, but I just only recently learned about you and Aiko-san and wanted to meet you." Her words came with surprising ease.

The woman bobbed her bowed head up and down as she listened. Then without the usual preliminary amenities that the Japanese usually exchange when they meet for the first time, she said in a clear lilting voice, "*Zannen nagara*, unfortunately, *Ai-chan* is gone. She passed away exactly eleven years ago last month."

Kato-san spoke simply, matter-of-factly, without a trace of sorrow or rancor in her voice. Emiko felt numbed but not surprised. Until that moment she had not thought about what she would have done had she found Aiko. What would they have said to each other? What would she have proposed?

"She was not quite thirty years old when she died," the woman continued. "Shortly after your father's death, I had this trouble with my back and was bedridden for more than a year. Ai-chan worked at the hot springs while taking care of me. Every day she took me there for treatments in a bicycle sidecar. When I was well enough to take care of myself, she went to Tokyo to look for a job. She prospered there and seemed very happy. They say she died of a sudden illness."

It sounded like a dramatic recitation, dispassionately and beautifully rendered. Emiko sat and waited for more, but the small, frail woman made a motion to stand up as if the subject were closed and said quietly, "*Otera in iki masho ka?* Shall we go to the temple?"

"*Hai*," Emiko consented readily because she felt she needed more time with Kato-san, but more than that, she assumed that the woman was suggesting they go to visit Aiko's shrine. The suggestion seemed just right. She had come all this distance. She should at least pay her respects.

The girl appeared at the doorway as if she had been summoned and leaned down to help Kato-san to her feet. Emiko realized for the first time that the woman was severely disabled and was unable to straighten up her body. Emiko was reminded of the illustrations in Japanese fairy tales of stooped grandmothers leaning on their canes. When they stepped out into the front entrance the girl said, "Excuse me, I will bring your *geta*. It is very wet outside."

Kato-san reached over to grab the handle of the baby carriage frame and released the girl's arm.

"She is getting them from my house, my parent's house, in the back. That is my nephew's daughter. She has been such a great help."

The girl returned with the *geta*, helped Kato-san into them and excused herself. Once out on the front walk, Emiko looked back and saw that the stepping stones the girl was sweeping when she arrived led to a small house which was completely dwarfed by the new one, built on what must have been a front lawn. That was where Aiko wrote those letters, she thought, where those bundles of letters came from.

Kato-san led the way pushing the baby carriage frame before her. The metal frame was rusting badly, but the wheels were still intact and sturdy enough to serve as a walker. There was enough traction on the tires even on the somewhat muddy rainwashed path. She walked slowly, her right hand keeping a firm grip on the handle, and her left hand resting comfortably on her back. She craned her head sharply backward, looking over her left shoulder at Emiko almost at an upside-down angle. She carried on an easy conversation, occasionally stopping to exchange greetings with neighbors who were sweeping their front walks.

"I came back here and lived with my parents after I returned from America. I am very lucky. My nephew and his family take good care of me." She stopped to take a breath. "Your *Okaa-san*. Is she well?"

"Yes, thank you."

"I never meant her any harm," she said. "That life in America working at the restaurant was too hard for me. Your father was against it, but I came home." She stopped again. Emiko almost told her she did not need to talk just now but was at the same time eager for more information.

"I can't say that he cared about us more than he did your family. I only know that if it had not been for your father's money and packages of food and clothing after the war ended, we would have all starved. Aiko was born only a few months before the beginning of the war with America."

By this time, Emiko herself was bent over double in order to be face-to-face with Kato-san as she listened. She found herself bobbing her head as she walked, repeating over and over to this woman who asked for no pity, *suminasen deshita, suminasen deshita*. She wasn't apologizing, exactly, she said to herself as she became aware of her own posture; she was truly sorry that there had been so much suffering.

"We were very lucky," Kato-san was saying, "your father saw us through the most difficult times imaginable. Normally, a girl brings disgrace on her family by becoming a mistress of a married man and having a baby by him. But Aiko was a blessing. Because of your father, my parents, my brothers and their families were saved." Talking and walking was becoming difficult for Kato-san. They stopped to rest, but they were already at the front gate of the temple.

They rested on the bench after removing their footwear and placing them in the small boxes at the entrance. The "walker" with its muddy wheels had to be left there. Kato-san took Emiko's elbow and leaned heavily on it. They walked down an aisle past hundreds of tiny identical shrines piled on top of each other. Each shrine contained a small ceramic incense pot on red lacquered stands. What Emiko assumed to be family names were inscribed on glittering gilt boards elaborately framed. Kato-san kept up her running comments and her voice echoed on the bare beams above them.

"Ai-chan is now with her grandparents. She should be at peace, finally. I'm sure of it." Emiko felt very much at ease in the temple. There was something about the rhythmic patterns of the shrines in rows, in columns, that was calming to the senses.

They stopped in front of the family shrine, lit a match to thin stems of incense, and placed them in the incense pots. Kato-san started to kneel down with some difficulty and pulled Emiko down beside her. They both bowed their heads and offered a silent prayer. Still clinging to Emiko's arm, Kato-san could raise only one hand in prayer. Then looking up at the shrine she spoke in her clear bell-like voice that her father surely must have fallen in love with, "Here is your *Nesan*, your big sister, Ai-chan. Isn't that nice? She has come all the way from America just to see you. Aren't you fortunate?" Then turning to Emiko she asked, "Emiko-san, wouldn't you like to talk to Ai-chan?" Emiko managed a smile but shook her head. No, she would not. Suddenly it all felt too maudlin to her, and the incense was making her ill. She would have got up and run out of the temple if Kato-san had not had a firm grip on her elbow.

"Then will you please tell her father that we are doing well when you return to America?" The suggestion surprised Emiko.

"Her father's ashes are in America among the Christians," Kato-san said. She added slowly, "I know this is very forward of me and a great imposition, but do you think your mother might possibly consent to having half of his ashes brought here to this temple so that he can be with Ai-chan?"

What an extraordinary idea! It took Emiko a few seconds to respond. She could only say, "*Kiite mimasu*, I will ask." Remembering her mother's plaintive expression sitting at the kitchen table, Emiko thought for a flickering second that she might say yes, that her mother might like that; but she did not. Instead, she fumbled in her shoulder strap bag, pulled out the brown envelope and offered it to Kato-san who squinted at it intently and tilted her head toward the shrine. Emiko placed the letter beside the gilt frame, bowed her head again for a brief moment. She helped Kato-san to her feet and the two women slowly made their way back to the entrance.

山田えツエ

III. RESISTING

I LEARNED TO SEW
☐

How can I say this?
My child
My life is nothing
There is nothing to tell

My family in Japan was too poor
to send me to school
I learned to sew
always I worked to help my family
when I was seventeen years old
and no one made marriage offer
a friend in our village who was going
to Hawaii a picture bride
said to me
Come with me

I did not want to
my parents did not want me to
my picture was sent to a stranger anyway
a young man's photograph and letter came
I was already seventeen years old
I went to the island of Hawaii to marry
this photograph.

This man came to the boat
he was too shy to talk to me
the Immigration man said to him
Here
sign here for her
He walked away
The Immigration man came to me
Don't you have relatives in Hawaii?

I said
Yes I have that man who will marry me
He said
Go back to Japan on the next boat
I said
I will wait here for my man
The Immigration man said
No
your man is not coming back
he told me he does not want you
he said you are too ugly for him
why don't you go back to Japan
on the next boat?
I said
No
I am not going back
I am staying here

>Just
>A minute
>My child
>Put that pen down
>Do not write this
>I never told this to anybody
>Not even to my oldest son, your father
>I now tell this story
>To you first time in sixty years

I sat at Immigration for a long time
people came and people went
I stayed
I could not see the sky
I could not see the sun
outside the window
I saw a seaweed forest
the crickets made scraping sounds
the geckos went tuk tuk tuk
sometimes a gecko would come into my room
but I was not afraid to talk to it
it came and it went as it pleased

I was thinking about Urashima Taro
you know the story?
Urashima disappeared into the sea
lived in the undersea world
married a beautiful princess
returned to his village
a very old man
I was thinking
I will leave this place
only when I am an old lady.

Pretty soon the Immigration man came to me
We found your cousin
In two weeks a cousin I met once
in Japan came for me
I stayed with him and his wife until
my cousin found a job for me
I worked doing housework
I did this for one year

My cousin found a husband for me
he was a merchant
we had a small store
and sold dry goods
my husband died after three sons
your father, my oldest son was six years old
I could not keep the store
I could not read
I could not write
the only thing I knew how to do was sew

I took the cloth from our store
sewed pants and undergarments
put the garments on a wooden cart
ombu the baby on my back
we went from plantation to plantation
sold my garments to the workers
I was their only store
sewed more garments at night
I did this for five years.

Your father grew up to love study and books
my friends called him the professor
he was then eleven years old
I said to him you need a father
He said I want to go to college
I said to him I will marry any man you say
I will marry any man
who will send you to college

One day he came home and said
I went to a matchmaker and
found a husband for you
he will marry a widow with three sons
will send them to college
he is a plantation foreman.

I married this man.

By and by my oldest son went away
to college in Honolulu
but my husband's boss told him
I need workers
your three sons must work
on my plantation like the others.
My husband said
No
He kept his word to my oldest son
and lost his job.

After that we had many hard times
I am nothing
know nothing
I only know how to sew
I now sew for my children and grandchildren
I turn to the sun every day of my life
pray to Amaterasu Omikami
for the health and
education of my children
for me that is enough

      My child
      Write this
      There   take your pen
      There   write it
      Say that I am not going back
      I am staying here

山田えツェ

JENI'S COMPLAINT
□

Grandma is parcelling out
her possessions on
my wedding day:
    Here
    you take mah jong set
    tiles old and yellow
    but real
    ivory
    and real bamboo
    I diesoon
    Don 't need.

Grandma told her friend:
    Fourteen grandchildren
    first time together
    in twelve years
    my three sons and daughter
    at my granddaughter's wedding
    my first her first
    maybe the last.

Phil and I
are rewriting our vows
with my Uncle Mike:
Don't wear your collar Uncle
It looks too Catholic
We want it ecumenical
And not too many prayers please
But make them Judeo-Christian.

Uncle Tosh is directing the boys:
>Have the guests park along
>Turtlerock Drive.

Aunt Elsie is arranging the table:
>Where shall we put the anthiriums
>from Hawaii?

Someone breaks a glass in the kitchen
and Dad calls out:
>Watch out don't anyone
>come in here with bare feet.

Grandma is offering a ceremonial
samurai sword to Steve who is listening
to Uncle Tosh's parking instructions:
>This was your grandpa's
>See handle real mother of pearl
>very old
>very expensive
>I diesoon
>Don't want

Uncle Mike is saying to Phil and me
>If you throw out everything
>you don't need a priest
>you can marry yourselves.

Grandma is offering her fancy
tea set to Hedi:
      I bring this from Japan
      before the war
      Now these days
      can't buy
      You marry soon
      to nice Japanese boy?
      Take this
      I alone now
      I diesoon
      Can't use.

No Grandma
not now
not now
later
later.

山田ミツヱ

PLAYING CARDS WITH THE JAILER

☐

A brief metallic sound
jars
the quiet night air
hangs
in my ears.

I am playing cards with the jailer
who shifts his ample body in his chair
while I fix my smile on his cards
waiting

My eyes unfocused on the floor
behind him where a set of keys spiderlike
begins to creep slowly across the room.
Come on come on your play I say
To distract him I tap the table
Wait.

With a wide gesture
he picks up the keys
hangs them back on the hook
Yawns.

The inmates will keep trying will keep trying
Their collective minds pull the keys
only halfway across the room each time
The world comes awake in the morning to a stupor
My brown calloused hands guard two queens and an ace
My polished pink nails shine in the almost light
I have been playing cards with jailers
for too many years.

山
田
ミ
ツ
エ

DROWNING
IN MY OWN LANGUAGE
☐

My world is a brain
shaped island encrusted
from decades of crevices
rumblings seethe
without cracking

the open half
of me is
sinking on a small
land mass into the sea

as I watch rows
of animated people in
white suits
converse on dry
land inches away with
out seeing
me single-handed
clawing
my way up grasping
exposed root ends
crying
out
slow
ly
still
sinking

tas-keh-tehhh

wrong language
the line of white heels
in half
moons over my head
fade away
waves scoop
more land
I look
round-eyed fish
in the mouth

helllllllllllp

still
wrong language

I will come up for air
in another language
all my own.

MRS. HIGASHI IS DEAD

☐

She carries in my lunch on a white wicker basket bed tray promptly at 12:00 noon, gently helps me to sit up, sets the tray firmly in front of me just as she has done the day before, the day before that and the day before that and asks, "*Korede de* oh righto?"

"Oh yes, thanks. That's just fine," I say cautiously. The sciatica that had me writhing in pain has finally become tolerable, and I am able to sit up comfortably for the first time in four days.

These few days in bed have been a revelation for me. As I lay flat on my back in my bedroom trying to distract my mind from the pain, I have been listening to my mother slam cupboard doors shut. I follow her footsteps as she stomps about my kitchen engaged in a flurry of multiple chores. I learn, for instance, that she prepares separate breakfasts for my husband and each one of the children and calls out each order, "two egisu ando bacon," like a short order cook, while packing their pre-ordered lunches in their lunch boxes. Funny, when I do the cooking they never complained to me about the same-menu-for-the-whole-family meals on weekends. All the while I hear the washer and dryer running in the laundry room adjoining the kitchen. There is a great deal of shouting in both Japanese and English as she pushes my two sons out the door to school and accompanies June, my preschool daughter, to the curb to await the school bus. I hear my sons calling out amidst a gale of laughter, "Gramma, etee Mighty Mouse yo."

It was the children's version of the proper Japanese expression "*Itte mairi masu yo*" when taking leave. They repeat spiritedly, "Gramma, etee Mighty Mouse yo," and my mother responds, "*Itte rashai.*" She has accepted their indecorous attitude toward the ceremony she has insisted they observe. I feel a twinge of regret that I have been missing these rituals every morning. Usually on a typical working day, I am out of the house to my job, a thirty mile commute, before anyone else in the family. This morning the children forget that I am home in bed and dash out of the house without saying goodbye to me.

I notice that my mother is, as she probably has been from six o'clock this morning, fully dressed from the top of her carefully coiffed and netted hair to her nylon stockinged feet in low-heeled shoes. She never flaps about in slippers like most Issei women.

As I lift the lids off the hot rice and soup bowls on the tray, my mother stands over me and says cheerfully in Japanese, "Sa-a, we have to build up one's strength and get back to work, neh? *Tottemo erai shigoto dakara.*"

It occurs to me that she has been speaking to me in a polite and patronizing tone in Japanese these past few days while giving short and direct commands to the children in her own version of English, "put 'em away," "hari appu."

Perhaps because the Japanese language permits her to speak without pronouns, she can make her efforts at coaxing me back to health sound as if we are doing it together. The expression *erai shigoto dakara* sounds ambiguous to me. Should I take it to mean that I do such important work or that my work is too hard for me?

"Have you noticed the difference in the way she talks to us?" I asked my husband the night before. I was in a mood for conversation for a change. "I mean, to me and the children, especially."

"Don't worry about it," my husband said. "Anyway, she's become even more compulsive about cooking and cleaning around here, that's for sure," he said, as if that explained anything.

I am not particularly hungry, but she has arranged the tray so elegantly that I dare not tell her. I slowly work on the bowl of brown rice, miso soup with tofu, a vegetable nishime, and seaweed sunomono while my mother tells me she's been reading in a Japanese nutrition book that miso kills germs, brown rice and tofu give you strength, and seaweed cleans out your system. In a few minutes she looks at her watch and says "It's 12:30; time for the mail."

I had forgotten how much my mother's life used to be run by the clock when I was growing up. We have had no problems the past five years with her running the household during my normal working hours and my taking over responsibilities the minute I walk into the door with an armful of groceries after work. During these past four days, instead of retreating into her room after dinner to watch television, she has been supervising the children's study time, bath time and bedtime by the clock. Naturally, they are protesting, though rather meekly, it seems to me.

"Mom, why is Gramma making us take a bath so early? We still hafta do our homework," and my mother would chime in amiably before I could say anything at all, "Oh, so-o? Do you sink so? Oh righto," but she would continue to draw the bathwater every evening right on her own schedule for each of the children anyway.

Interesting, I think to myself, how she just goes about her duties without listening to anybody, and we all seem to fall right in line.

In fact, the timing of the events in our lives the past five years seemed perfectly attuned: my father's death, my daughter's birth, my mother's move to join us, and my returning to work. She was somewhat tentative at first about thinking in terms of settling down "permanently" with us but adjusted quickly. My husband and I were amazed at her transformation from a crestfallen widow to a vigorously energetic mother's helper. After my father's death, it took a whole year of persuasion before she finally sold her house and made this major move. It was too difficult for her to divest herself of her furniture and thirty-six years of accumulated possessions, so we persuaded her to bring them with her and stored most of the furniture in our double garage. She came and put my "much-neglected house" in sparkling order. It was not our original intention to "use" her as a housekeeper, but it seemed to be exactly what she enjoyed doing the most, we reasoned. She and I fell into the division of labor quite naturally and happily without discussion. I often spoke to my envious friends of my "perfect wife" at home who made my coffee every morning and sometimes packed my lunch along with the children's. Until I started working, I had not realized how much I was straining at the leash at home.

"She really needed to be needed!" my husband and I said to each other with satisfaction.

Just as I am about to finish my lunch, my mother returns with a small stack of mail and places it on the tray. I flip through the mail, pick out the one personal piece among the junk mail, and impatiently tear open the envelope.

"Ouch," I suck on the painful paper slit between my thumb and forefinger. My mother shakes her head, "*Sosokka shii hito,*" she says, laughing. When I was a child, this phrase thrown in my direction whenever I dropped a dish or scratched the furniture, used to scrape a nerve ending and make me shudder, but these days we say it to each other after one of us stumble over her own feet, the way people say *gesunheit* after a sneeze.

"Like mother like daughter," I say cheerfully, for we both now know that she herself never moves slowly while doing her chores and always manages to gash, rip, or stab herself. I unfold the contents of the envelope and read the letter to myself, eager for any news from the outside. It is a short handwritten note, xeroxed, from an old friend.

"Dear Sister, I'm at the end of my rope, (read that, funds). Haven't worked for three months. Landlady breathing down my emaciated neck. If you have a few dollars you will not be using for a while (read that, about a year) can you send them my way? Pronto-like? Luvya, Dolores."

My mother is trying to look busy smoothing out my bed covers, tucking the ends of the blankets under the mattress. I let out an appreciative hoot, "What a character!" and impulsively blurt out a reasonable translation of the letter's contents into Japanese.

"Who is she?" my mother asks suspiciously.

"Oh, one of my favorite people, an absolutely beautiful, wacko, Black woman I knew in graduate school. Since nobody will hire her to do the kind of work she wants to, she has been out of work and needs money to hold her over."

When I am working, I am able to keep the different parts of my life compartmentalized: the professional, the personal, and the domestic. Most of the time my conversations with my mother revolve around domestic affairs: what to have for dinner, how to remove that spot on the rug, and what to do about the children (including my husband) hiding dirty socks under their beds. She only knows my close friends casually for I rarely talk about them with her. She would consider Dolores, to whom I am a kindred soul, not a wife, mother, daughter, or office manager, to be one of my "brash" friends. Now that I am in bed and she is watching my every move and mood, I feel obliged to share this friend with her. I regret it immediately, for she shakes her head disapprovingly, that familiar motherly shake.

"*Mah, haji shirazu.*"

I am startled to hear that expression I had not heard from my mother for a long time. I feel defensive about my friend, Dolores.

"Why? Why is it shameful of her?" I ask defiantly.

My mother's words remind me of Mrs. Stack's fresh-baked breads every Monday and Friday morning. I would be playing in our backyard alone while my brothers were in school, staying close to the low hedge that separated our backyards. When Mrs. Stack eventually appeared at her screen door, I would run to the bottom of the stairs and call out boldly, "Hi Mrs. Stack, is it ready?" and begin climbing up without invitation. She would hold the screen door open with one hand and gently push me into her kitchen with the other. There was the familiar faint whiff of sweat from her ample body, but once I entered her kitchen, the wonderful aroma of fresh-baked bread enveloped me. Her kitchen walls and floors were several shades of dark woods with the grains running in different directions. The woods on the floor were highly polished but worn, and I could feel the uneven grains under my thin-soled shoes. The counters were stacked with glass jars full of colorful fruits and vegetables.

A huge stove with a shiny black door, a large gold letter "A" imprinted on the front of it, dominated this kitchen. Mrs. Stack would tear off a crusty piece from one of the round loaves cooling on the heavy kitchen table and lumber over to me. Her dimpled hand felt soft and warm as I cupped my hands to receive the bread.

"Now run along, Little One, before Mama sees you."

I would feel a glow from being included among her many grandchildren who were all "Little Ones" to her. My mother was not much for affectionate names. I was *Aki-chan* until my baby brother was born when I was four years old. From then on she talked to me through my baby brother and referred to me as *Nesan*, big sister, "*Nesan* will do such and such." Or she called me A-ki-ko punctuating the harsh k's, especially when giving out orders or scolding me.

I would descend the short flight of stairs on Mrs. Stack's back porch, carefully cradling the piece of warm bread in my hands hoping my mother would be upstairs caring for the baby. Invariably she would call me from the kitchen window. I would come to her very slowly, opening our back door just enough for me to squeeze through, hiding the piece of bread behind me. She would be standing at the kitchen sink looking out the window,

"A-ki-ko, *Nani shiteru no?*" she would ask as if she didn't know, as if this were not an every Monday and Friday ritual.

"Nothing. Nothing, Mama."

Then she would look at me, her glance following the curve of my arm looking right through me at the offending piece of bread behind my back.

"*Mah,*" she would exclaim as if she made a surprising discovery, "*haji shirazu. Mata jama shiteru.*"

Haji and *jama*, the two words that repeatedly appeared in different contexts in my young life. How many times had she told me that it was shameful to bother other people? Had she not told me not to *jama* the white lady next door? For a long time I'd associated *jama* with jam, jam to put on my delicious bread. I would sit on the back steps and in spite of my guilt feelings, would enjoy Mrs. Stack's still-warm home-made bread even without the jam.

I hold up Dolores' letter, "Why," I repeat, "why is this shameful?"

"*Soredemo,*" my mother gropes about for words, "it's the way your friend asks, so shamelessly, so flippantly."

How do I tell her that that's exactly what I love about her?

"Oh, so it's *haji* because she's not asking humbly? Should she apologize all over the place like the way the Isseis do?"

It sounds more insulting than I intend, but she does not take it personally. She simply says defensively that that's certainly better than begging so openly.

"Then how about those priests who used to come to your older sister's house every morning to beg for alms? That seemed pretty open to me."

I am now determined to follow this discussion through and this remote memory out of those brief early years I spent in Japan suddenly surfaces out of nowhere. Instinctively, I have decided that this subject is safer than Mrs. Stack's bread and many other childhood memories associated with *haji* and *jama*, words which ruled those years so powerfully.

My mother gives me that "you-Nisei-understand-nothing" look and says forcefully, "What are you talking about? Of course, there is a world of difference!"

I remember the gentle tinkling bell that used to awaken me every morning in my mother's home town where I had been sent when I was ten years old to learn proper Japanese ways. I used to jump out of my futon every morning at the sound of the bell, re-tie the belt attached to my kimono and run out of my room. At the same time my aunt would shuffle out of her room and wait in the corridor with a fistful of coins extended towards me. I would take the coins from her hand and bolt toward the front entrance. The itinerant priest standing very erect in his flowing robe with a long staff in one hand and a bell in the other never failed to pique my curiosity. His face would be hidden behind a deep straw hat but I could tell by his slim tapered hands and his slight stature that he was very young. He reminded me of an old painting my mother had in the hallway in our house in America, of a shepherd in a long robe with a crooked staff in one hand watching over his flock of sheep. I would drop the coins in his cloth bag slung over his shoulder. He would bow curtly and disappear into the street, as the sound of his chanting voice accompanied by the tinkling bell lingered behind.

My mother sees that I have finished eating. She sets the tray aside on the dresser and plumps out my pillows. I sink back into them and tell her that on one occasion I asked *Obasan* why such young priests spent their whole days going from house to house like beggars.

"*Mah, haji kaku!*" my mother exclaims.

"*Obasan* said the same thing to me! There's that word again, *haji*."

My mother abruptly picks up the wicker tray and says, "June and the boys will be home soon. Time to prepare the snacks."

Prepare the snacks? What is there to prepare, I wonder as I lean over to turn on the radio. In half an hour she returns and resumes the conversation as if she had never left. She blurts out impatiently, "*Doshite wakaranai no kane.* The priests arent't begging. They give something back; they pray for our health and good fortune.

"So that's it. They hold themselves up with great pride because of that. No humility there. They ask, receive, and accept, all without ceremony." I try to bring us back to Dolores' letter.

Just then we hear the preschool bus out front and June's rapid footsteps in the house. June comes running into my bedroom with a handful of papers and spreads them out on my bed with running commentaries on the figures in her drawings. It occurs to me that the one reason why my mother and I can never have discussions that are halfway serious is because we are always being interrupted by the children. June turns to her grandmother, "Gramma, I'm hungry. What do we have for a snack?" As they leave the room, I overhear my mother telling June to first say "hello" to Grandpa, change her clothes, and don't forget to "put'em away." Without a word, June runs into her grandmother's room apparently to say "hello" to her grandfather's photograph on my mother's dresser. Although my mother has given up keeping a Buddhist shrine of her ancestors in the house after I reminded her years ago that it was inappropriate for a Christian to persist in this Buddhist ritual, she still has not given up the practice of giving offerings of food to the photograph of her parents and my father on her dresser. She has the children, June at least, observing this ritual of paying respects to their ancestors as a matter of course before getting their after-school snacks.

I listen to June's footsteps as she races through her grandmother's room to pay her respects to Grandpa, into her own room to change, and to the kitchen for a snack. Bang! She has already gone outdoors to play. A few minutes later I hear her shouting at the front door.

"Gramma, is it okay for Mrs. Clark to give me a lollipop?"

Mrs. Clark from across the street is my children's Mrs. Stack. Instead of fresh-baked bread on her kitchen table, Mrs. Clark keeps a supply of colorful lollipops in a glass jar.

"Shame on you, Junko," my mother scolds, "Grandma make you nice fruit snack. Why you *jama* the white lady? Grandma tell you don't *baza* the white lady." She translates *jama* into her own brand of English for greater emphasis. "Shame on you" doesn't sound quite as belittling as *haji shirazu*. My daughter, instead of withering under my mother's words as I would have done at her age, replies, "But Gramma, she *wants* me to bother her. She *likes* to give me things. She *enjoys* me." Bang!

This child and my mother are a comedy team. June was born a year after my mother's arrival. By then both boys were spending full days in school, and my mother was beginning to feel less useful around the house.

"It's a good thing we gave her June to keep her busy and happy," my husband and I had said as I prepared to go back to work three months later. She is the only grandchild who can get away with talking back to her grandmother, give back "as good as she takes," as my husband would say. When my mother tells the children in the morning, "Put your sweater on, it's cold outside," the boys would give in reluctantly, but June would snap back, "Why should I put a sweater on just because you're cold, Gramma? If you're cold, *you* put a sweater on!" and march off into the cool morning in her short-sleeved cotton dress.

I hear my mother in June's room. Through the common wall between our room and June's closet, I hear the sliding closet door opening and coat hangers clanging noisily. In a few minutes my mother appears at the doorway with an armful of clothes.

"Look at this! Your daughter left these strewn all over the floor in her room!"

I say in mock surprise, "Oh no, she didn't put'em away! Why don't you do what I do? Just close her door so you won't have to look at it." My mother's complaints about having to pick up after all of us have become so constant that we hardly hear them anymore. My way of dealing with my children's sloppy habits has been to joke about them, but I see that at the moment she is not in the mood for light-hearted bantering, and she launches into one of her tirades in Japanese, "Mama's trying to help you bring your children up right, but you're no help. Mama's doing everything by herself, but no one is grateful! *Hitottsu mo kansha shite nai!*"

This is more than her usual everyday grumbling about our lack of cooperation. She never used the word *kansha*, or lack of it, before. There is an intensity to her voice. I try to mollify her with my standard Dr. Spock-like response. She should let the children assume responsibilities for themselves, I tell her, or they will never learn. The problem with her is that she always does too much for them and then complains that they have not learned to take care of themselves.

"Why is it Mama's fault suddenly?" she is getting wound up now. "I am not the servant here, but I have been serving and serving."

I feel my sciatic pain returning, but I say with equal passion, "That's exactly the problem with you, Mother. You are always giving and giving too much!"

"Aruhito wa morau bakari!" she shouts back.

The outburst takes us both by surprise. Am I one of those people? Do I only take and take without giving back? Then my mother abruptly changes her tone and says softly, *"Ageru nomo, morau nomo, onnashi."* Her words sink in slowly. Giving and taking, they are the same.

"Toki ni yotte?" I ask, qualifying her remark. In some cases? She nods.

"Do you remember my good friend Mrs. Higashi?" It is now Mother's turn to bring up an old long-forgotten memory.

I was twelve years old. I must have just returned from school with an armful of schoolbooks. I found my mother weeping by the telephone, both fists pounding on the triangular telephone table nestled in the corner of the hallway. I was about to sneak up the stairs because this behavior, coming from a mother who was always coolly composed, embarrassed me. I had never seen her display such violent emotions before. When she saw me, she did not try to hide her tears; she simply said, *"Higashi no okusan shinde shimatta."*

I suck in my breath, "How did she die?"

Mrs. Higashi was the widow of our egg man who lived three blocks down the street from us. Mr. Higashi, who died the year before, used to drive out to the dairy farm and then deliver fresh eggs to us three times a week. After his death, my father and a few of the neighbors tried to help his widow and six small children by picking up eggs for her in turns since she did not drive. In our neighborhood, she was a familiar sight, pulling a child's wagon up and down the street with egg cartons piled on it. It looked to me as if they were having fun, the baby sitting in the wagon and older ones pulling or pushing it. They seemed to be managing well.

But Mrs. Higashi had turned on the gas stove in her kitchen and killed herself and her children.

"Yes of course. I remember Mrs. Higashi. Very vividly, in fact." I am still picturing the six small children, the wagon, the egg cartons.

Erakatta!" Mother says quietly. I am pondering the multiple implications of this expression: tired, difficult, great, noble, admirable. "Life was hard" for Mrs. Higashi? "Life was difficult" for Mother too? "Mrs. Higashi was noble" because she suffered alone? "She was admirable" because she killed herself?

Mother begins to straighten out the sundry items on my bed stand as she talks.

"Those days. The Issei women were not as lucky as you are today. There was nobody to help us. No family. She had all those little children. Only some help from a few friends. Not enough. The rest of us had our hands full too. She was proud. She didn't want to *jama* anybody. She couldn't bring *haji* on her family by begging, could she? *Higashi no okusan shinde shimatta.*"

"*Shinde shimatta.* That's what you said when you first told me about Mrs. Higashi's suicide. Isn't that an odd way of putting it?" I ask. It was as if death came to Mrs. Higashi, or as if death was simply a state of being.

"*Mattaku sohyo.* Mrs. Higashi is dead," Mother says with finality, "because she didn't think there was any other way out."

I am beginning to understand that it is more than the differences in our languages that keep us, Mother and me, at a certain distance.

"Do you know," I tell her, "that in English there would be no other way of talking about her suicide except to say 'she killed herself' as if she willed it on herself, even if she didn't?" I am thinking of the phrase "committing suicide," as if suicide were making a commitment.

"What your friend did," Mother says pointing to Dolores' letter on the bed, "that would be hard for a Japanese woman to do. *Omoi naoshitara, kanshin da neh?*"

"You mean, you changed your mind about her? Now you think Dolores is *kanshin?*" I want to make sure we are talking about the same thing. The word she used before, *kansha,* means grateful, but this time she means *kanshin,* admirable. I can't find the appropriate way in Japanese to tell Mother that, in a way, both words apply to her: we are grateful to her, and she is *kanshin* too. I say simply, "Yes, it would be hard for me too, but I do admire Dolores for her spunk."

We are both quiet for a few moments. We hear the boys at the front door, "Gramma, we're home!"

Mother responds automatically, "*Hai,* here, in your mother's room," and is about to leave the room.

I sit up with some effort and reach for the checkbook and pen in the bed stand drawer.

"Mama was thinking," she turns and says almost casually, "do you think you and the children will be able to fend for yourselves a little after you are well?"

I set the checkbook aside.

She continues, "Mama was thinking of moving into an apartment. Not too far away."

I let my feet dangle on the edge of the bed and look up feeling absolutely released.

"Of course, Mama will come to help sometimes. But I want my own place and have my own things around me."

I see that Mother, now halfway out the door to greet the boys, looks as though she is at peace with herself.

"Mama wa kakugo shitayo."

Kakugo, yes, that's the word: ready, prepared, resolved, determined.

"Are you sure?"

"Yes."

"If you're really sure, it would be wonderful for you. We will help you with the rent."

IV. CONNECTING

MY COUSIN

□

       the failed kamikaze pilot
who lived to miss only three fingers
on his right hand
offers me a sip of California wine
in his trim garden.
He, pacific, a giant
among dwarfed trees
one hand resting
on the arm of
an imported chair
a clear stemmed glass poised
between his thumb and pinkie
answers a question I could not
ask for thirty years:

        Of course I don't
        I don't really believe
        "it is sweet and fitting
        to die for one's country."

It is evening and the canary clears its throat.
I leave among cricket sounds in the woods.

SUBURBIA IN FULL BLOOM
☐

*Among the abused women in the United States, at least
one-quarter of all attacks are made on wives who are
pregnant, according to sociologist Dr. Richard J. Gelles.*

A neighbor and I were
out for a stroll under
massive maples
lining the boulevard
Both pregnant for the
first time,
how proud we were.

"Blessed are you among women
and blessed is the fruit of your womb."

Into the tunnel of trees
dropped the town bully,
a seven year old boy,
like a dancer not
missing a step
trotted backwards before us
nodding at one and
the other

"Man, ya sure gotchaselfs fucked up good."

We looked
the other's image reflected
in each other's eyes
and felt
blessed
no more.

The boy
now a young man
is a collector
of assorted parts
has lead pieces inside
his head
some day to explode
inside any woman and says
sure I do
a woman's like
Mt. Everest
she's there.

Now his wife is pregnant
I hear
and neighbor boy
the town bully
sees red.

"Blessed are you among women
and blessed is the fruit of your womb."

THE CLUB

☐

He beat me with the hem of a kimono
worn by a Japanese woman
this prized
painted
wooden statue
carved to perfection
in Japan or maybe Hong Kong.

She was usually on display
in our living room atop his bookshelf
among his other overseas treasures
I was never to touch.
She posed there most of the day
her head tilted
her chin resting lightly
on the white pointed fingertips
of her right hand
her black hair
piled high on her head
her long slim neck bared
to her shoulders.
An invisible hand
under the full sleeve
clasped her kimono
close to her body
its hem flared
gracefully around her feet.

That hem
made fluted red marks
on these freckled arms
my shoulders
my back.
That head
inside his fist
made camel
bumps
on his knuckles
I prayed for her
that her pencil thin neck
would not snap
or his rage would be unendurable.
She held fast for me
didn't even chip or crack.

One day, we were talking
as we often did the morning after.
Well, my sloe-eyed beauty, I said
have you served him enough?
I dared to pick her up with one hand
I held her gently by the flowing robe
around her slender legs.
She felt lighter than I had imagined.
I stroked her cold thighs
with the tips of my fingers
and felt a slight tremor.

I carried her into the kitchen and wrapped her
in two sheets of paper towels.
We're leaving
I whispered
you and I
together.

I placed her
between my clothes in my packed suitcase.
That is how we left him
forever.

山田ミツヱ

ENOUGH

☐

I see my body metaphored by
peace-loving
young-blooded
eco-minded
oversexed
male poets.
They protest that
a forest of my pubic hair
prolific, fertile, enticing
is cut down
mercilessly macheted.
They wail that I
an ocean hiding huge
reservoirs of active oil
am pumped, drummed, depleted.
They groan that I
a small Asian nation
with a frail body wedged between
continents is ravaged over
and over.

I sit in this privileged circle
a lone woman
a lone Asian
with literal fingernails
digging into my palms
yellow blood oozing
to the floor.

FOR LAURA
WHO STILL HEARS THE GEESE
☐

When I heard you read your poem about the children
your images rubbed clean with right words
polished smooth for our fragile ears to savor
I said
>Don't tell me with worn words, Laura
>Show me
>Show me what you saw with your own eyes
>Tell me what you heard with your own ears.

I saw then in your face
the same searching look
the pinched face of that woman
I met in Japan
in another language
Mouthing clichés too
she said
>like hell on earth
>like a horrible nightmare
>like nothing you can imagine
>like everything you can imagine
>even then you will never know
>Hiroshima was a human junk heap.

Your words came in slow, measured tones
>I couldn't hear the children
>I couldn't hear their cries
>because of the geese.
and I jumped
>Geese?
>What geese?

You said
>
> All those geese the guards brought in
> to the square to beat
> while they marched
> marched the children
> into the ovens.
> I couldn't hear the children
> I only heard
> out of their open mouths
> the squawking geese sounds
> the beating wings sounds
> We were returning to our bunks
> after working all night
> all night
> I have no words
> No other words.

You said these words as I sat at the edge
of my seat waiting for you to show me
in precise diction
in sharp new images
in fresh vital language
what you saw
to let me live through your vision
that I might live too.

I will never forget your geese, Laura
but still I cannot feel the bodies
of those children that have left acid shadows
on your brain to burn and burn
I never can.

LETHE

☐

He said
"With my own eyes
I have seen them
watch their children's
skinny-ribbed bodies
beaten
bleeding in the streets
I knew then
I know now
they are not like us
who care
about life
liberty
and happiness."

In his tight pink skin
this veteran student
his lips a white line
flesh bulging in hard knobs over
his jaw bones
in the blue light
flailed at me across
the classroom distance
where I stood pinned
against the blackboard wall
a broken piece of chalk
in the palm of my hand.

Because I was silent then
the lesson for the day
still spills
over me
spewing
after this student
who has seen too much
or not enough.

Because I was silent then
those metal-rimmed glasses
hang pinned to the cork wall
his grey eyes fixed
while I stand before him
a broken piece of white chalk
in the palm of my hand.

山田ミツ工

MY HOME TOWN THIS EARTH
□

Imagine there is a future
where a tight ring of peace
like Saturn's collar
holds us all in
and there is no
space for war

Imagine there is a future
where my home town
this earth
is no longer
an experimental station
for nuclear wars

Imagine there is a future
where our psychic Geiger counters find
no clicking nightmares in the air

where no child
sees its mother's image
in pieces of charcoal
buried in the ground
where she was burned

where no mother cries
over her child's coffin
killed at war
killed in the war
killed by hate
killed by hunger

I lay my aging woman body
on this ground
spread eagled
reaching to four points
 of our common future
our shared pasts
and remember

we must make a future
for those for whom survival only
is not enough
we must make a future
for those so bereft in mind and spirit
they cannot imagine there is a future.

Imagine there is a future
for eyes
watching us here
watching us now
through the wrong end of a telescope.

山田ミツヱ

ESCAPE
□

Once upon a time I lived in a one-room apartment with a
mother and three brothers, no plumbing, and 8,000 friendly
neighbors to share our sagebrush lawn in the desert of Idaho.
Soon after the great war, I scaled the barbed wire fence and
sprung myself out into the open streets of New York City.

I shared a $35.00 a month fifth floor walk-up flat with two
roommates on Lower East Side Manhattan with one narrow
window. Our ice-box clung to the windowsill on two nails.
In the middle of our kitchen/sitting room sat a bathtub
covered with a white enameled top which doubled for a kitchen
counter and tripled for a dining table. Its rounded bottom
was propped up by four sturdy claws. To take a bath we
folded back one half of the rusty hinged cover, filled it
with hot water from a bucket on our two-burner gas range.
During the winter months, it was the warmest spot in our
apartment, that is, if two of us were willing to keep filling
it with hot water while the lucky one lounged in it like a
contented baby in a carriage. But one night the hinges on
our rotting wooden door failed to protect us from intruders
who thought we were the red light district.

I left, backed up into marriage and moved into a two-bedroom,
second floor garden apartment with central heating, a
courtyard with green grass and a scenic view of huge oil
drums from Con Edison. In three years the wind whipped
circles of dust in the bare courtyard, drunks blocked our
entrance to the building, Kitty Genovese was murdered in her
own hallway in neighboring Kew Gardens, and we imagined
someone someday dropping a bomb into one of the oil drums.

For the sake of our children we moved to the safety of the suburbs in California, with green grass, high walls, an inside garden called an atrium, a neighborhood watch, and a drug trade that stays underground where we cannot see it. We now live here like comfortable hermits while the wife of the president of us all declares war on drugs from her house surrounded by green grass, high walls, the Rose Garden and the Secret Service.

山田えつエ

FOR·PRISCILLA
☐

During the years you were in China we led undirected lives
until you sent us each disjointed sentences on strips of paper
and steered us together by remote control
while we read your jig-sawed letter.

Last Easter you brought my first experience of the Passover Seder
because, you said, I mustn't spend my Easter sick in bed.
You brought into my dining room the shankbone, roasted egg,
bitter-herbs, and turkey, baked boiled and spiced.
You marched in with your own team of out-of-town guests
and conducted our recitation from Ben Shahn's Haggadah.

Now night has fallen on the lids of your home on the hill
and on the ferns of hair in your walkway.
Strange heels clatter against the blue and white tiles
you laid on your floors with rubber-gloved hands, and
the black angry streak you marked on Laguna Canyon Road
is now muted by more drunken tires.

How shall we now celebrate next year's Easter/Passover
without your own homey brand of the Seder Table?
We will count the number of chairs around our table
...again and again.
Pockets of air will not be filled
with the warm shrill of your voice.

But Priscilla
the tracks you left with your poems will stay
to press my ears with your laughter and
now I must grow old for the both of us.

MASKS OF WOMAN

☐

I.

This is my daily mask
daughter, sister
wife, mother
poet, teacher
grandmother.

My mask is control
concealment
endurance
my mask is escape
from my
self.

II. (Noh mask of benign woman)

Over my mask
is your mask
of me
an Asian woman
grateful
gentle
in the pupils of your eyes
as I gesture with each
new play of
light
and shadow
this mask be
comes you.

But here
I shall remove
your mask
of me and
my daily mask
of me
like the used skin
of a growing reptile
it peels away
and releases

III. (Mask of Daruma, weighted toy-god)

Daruma
my mouth is a funnel
words implode within and
burst forth through an
inverted megaphone
my bulging eyes command
your attention
I am Daruma
push me
I will not stay
stare me down
I will not look away
dare me to laugh
it off
I will not wince
a smile.

Daruma moves
me to resist
Daruma defies me
to act and
I become

IV. (Mask of Onibaba, old witch)

Onibaba
old woman hag
watch Onibaba's
streaks of light
ages of my sorrows
glow through each
lentigo
my infrared rays
will pierce your
mask.

V. (Noh mask of benign woman)

This is my daily mask
daughter, sister
wife, mother
poet, teacher
grandmother
My mask is control
concealment
endurance
my mask is escape
from my
self.

山田えつエ

YOU TOO CAN LIVE COMFORTABLY WITHOUT GUILT
□

A woman in a floor length mink coat as quoted
in the New York Times:
"The animals my coat was made of were already dead."

I helped kill a thing today
that bleared before me
then framed
on my rear view eyeball
glistening red
like an old matted fur rug
it lay newly rolled
once more pressed
another stria
on this virgin road
well paved by corpses.

> Don't look back
> what can you do?
> Others were here before you
> move lock-spinning ahead
> or we'll never get there

We whirred on humming to wheels
We swarmed together with bravado
The red blister
finally fades

Anyway, the corpse I killed
was already dead.

1986

HAROLD AND THE PURPLE CRAYON
☐

for Aaron and Jason

One summer
I gave you
a huge box
of crayons

and unleashed a roll of butcher paper in the park
    unrolled it over the wooden bridge through the
        dried-up creek up the hills into the canyons

and said, LET'S DO THE WORLD BOYS!

You made scratchessquigglescircles
        facespigsalligators
        housestreesmoons
        thundercatsspacemen
        windowswindowswindows

I wanted you
to have everyting
but not too much of
everything the world
can give
almost everything
but not too much.
I was afraid.

The butcher paper unrolls over your bridge
through your creek along our hillside
into our canyons and by your woods,
and with your redbluegreenblackyellowpurple paints
a spattering brush that crosses borders
you have colored my world forever.

山田
えツ工

91

A MOTHER'S TOUCH

☐

The tether that held me to you
would not let us touch
stiff from old stories
of oceans crossed
family ties lost
failed childhood dreams

dreams spilled into mine
when the new baby came
you said don't touch
the baby will spoil
I watched every day
for signs of green
fuzz on his clean
soft skin

skinned to the bone
in the bathtub you scrubbed
me with hands roughened
washing bucketsful of diapers
and our long cotton stockings
with your muscular arms

arms never closed me in
for fear too much warmth
would spoil me green too
when the war came and
I moved away
your strong busy arms were
solace to a prison damaged husband

troubled friends and needy relatives
the tether kept stretching
weighted by more children
and grandchildren.

Today it is a silken strand
that cuts into the flesh
of my unlabored hands
as I hang on long enough
for the unborn
to hear your old stories
of oceans crossed
family ties lost
and failed dreams.

山田ミツエ

PRAYER FOR CHANGE

□

My mother's voice hummed
through
a haze of gauze

"Forgive me
I must now speak up
we give you
name unsuited
to you poison
your blood
make you sick.
We will our gods
to change your name
to simple name
then you will live
please open
your eyes see me
hear me
hear my prayer.

A man wants three sons
a woman needs
one daughter.

When you born
your father
find in black book
a name for girl child
beautiful
flowing
deep
waters
he said
for my only daughter
a delicate girl name
write it different
write it fancy
this way
Mi-tsu-ye

but you my child
never beautiful
for you only plain
name lucky to you
bring your health back
back to me."

Blue surgical sounds of
a mother's prayer.

山田ミツエ

ABOUT THE AUTHOR
□

All her life Mitsuye Yamada has been searching for her cultural heritage and discovered that it is here, within her: in her poetry, in her work with multicultural groups, and in her work for human rights. She was born in Kyushu, Japan, and spent her childhood in Seattle, Washington, until the outbreak of World War II when her family was removed to a concentration camp in Idaho.

She teaches in the Asian American Studies Program at the University of California, Irvine. In the past years since her retirement from Cypress College, she has been Writer-in-Residence at California State University, Fullerton; Visiting Professor at University of California, Los Angeles; and Artist-in-Residence in the M.F.A. Creative Writing Program at San Diego State University.

She is founder and coordinator of the MultiCultural Women Writers (MCWW). Her human rights work includes spreading human rights awareness in Third World countries through the International Development Committee of Amnesty International, U.S.A. and supporting political prisoners in the United States through the Interfaith Prisoner of Conscience Project (IPOC).

In 1982 she was the recipient of the Vesta Award from the Woman's Building of Los Angeles. In 1984 she was awarded a writer's residency from Yaddo. She and Nellie Wong are the subjects of a film, "Mitsuye and Nellie: Asian American Poets," which aired nationally on PBS in 1981.